Embroidery and Animals

Embroidery and Animals

Jan Messent

Best Wishes to Anne.
Jan Messent. 1984.

B. T. BATSFORD LTD. LONDON

ISBN 0 7134 4333 2

Typeset by Santype International Ltd., Salisbury
and printed in Great Britain by
R. J. Acford, Chichester
for the publishers
B. T. Batsford Ltd.
4 Fitzhardinge Street
London W1H 0AH

Contents

Acknowledgment

I would like gratefully to acknowledge the help and co-operation of all those who have so generously allowed me to use their embroideries and ideas to illustrate this book. Particular thanks go to Jan Beaney and her many students who chose, quite by coincidence, to take the same theme of animals for their year's work, much to my good fortune, and who went to so much trouble to help me photograph it.

Valerie Campbell-Harding was dragged, unprotesting, to a zoo where she patiently took photographs of unco-operative animals for me, and Kit Pyman gave me so much encouragement in my search for material while ferrying me to and fro.

Special thanks to my dear family for their interest, patience, help and willingness to accept my lesser role as housewife during the last year.

Introduction and Historical Survey

Textiles dating from 500 BC to the present day show clearly that the urge to represent living creatures, real or imaginary, seems to overtake us all at some stage in our search for design material. The varied interpretations of this subject in textiles, particularly embroidery, make a fascinating study, as the diversity of styles depends not only on the country of origin and its traditions but also on the function of the embroidered article, the technique used and the age and skill of the craftsman. It is also interesting to note the similarity of designs from cultures far apart in both distance and time. The Persian influence, for instance, has spread far and wide over much of Europe and is manifest in the double-headed eagle of Hungary, Russia, Poland, Greece, Germany and France. Men on horseback, reindeer and standing birds (especially peacocks) are other examples of similarly wide-spread designs which may mislead one into thinking that identification is simple.

Styles of design also vary in their degree of realism and abstraction. Animals in English Elizabethan embroideries, for example, show a simple realism, often humorous and always enchanting, while on the other hand one of the easily recognizable hallmarks of both Chinese and Japanese embroidery is the completely two-dimensional, highly decorative and sophisticated portrayal of animal life. Further refinements of the decorative style can be seen in the counted threads of European peasant embroidery and an even more stylized type of design in the semi-abstract Peruvian Paracas embroideries of 500 BC. Nowhere else is abstraction in textiles carried to such a high degree of sophistication as in the countries of the Americas, from the Chilcat Indians in the north to the Cuna Indians of Panama in Central America and the ancient cultures of Peru in the south.

One could say that, in many cases, the type of design is dictated to a large extent by the embroidery technique used, as for instance in the well-known patchwork quilts of the early American settlers where simple animal shapes were cut out of small pieces of fabric; on the other hand, some amazingly complex designs of centuries ago were executed in drawn-thread work and quilting which today would make even the most experienced embroiderer hesitate.

Equally exciting to discover is the scope of animal life covered by textile artists, which includes not only familiar and indigenous species but also the mythical and fantastic monsters to be seen in the heraldic work of the Middle Ages. Some creatures could only have been described verbally to the artist; Abigail Pett embroidered camels, spotted leopards and bewildered-looking lions, which she cannot possibly have seen, onto her bed-curtains in the seventeenth century. Extremely accurate insects, bats, rodents, reptiles, sea-creatures and mammals of every kind abound in embroidery; nothing, it seems, has ever been too lowly or too adventurous to be used in a design. Those with very little, or even no experience in designing have produced the most delightful creatures, as can be seen in the following illustrations. Their naïveté rarely detracts from their charm; on the contrary, one of the most famous of all embroideries, the Bayeux Tapestry, has errors such as missing legs and parts of equipment, but the overall effect is one of strong rhythms and well balanced pattern.

In the chapters which follow, I hope you will be entirely convinced that, like the embroiderers who worked at the Bayeux Tapestry in the eleventh century, everyone is capable of creating a lively and interesting design from animal life. Although they were probably amateurs, their work has been admired for over 900 years; I hope that, with the aid of this book, you will be able to do at least as well.

It is inevitable that some readers, hoping to find a potential design for a particular animal, will be disappointed not to find it, or perhaps in a form unsuitable for their purposes. The subject is so large that omissions are unavoidable. Some animals have been excluded simply because the author has found it incredibly difficult to find any design points in their favour, and has included others more than once because of their abundance of decorative qualities and their universal popularity. This applies to my own favourite animal, the horse, for which piece of self-indulgence I apologize (though I have reason to believe I am not alone).

So many embroiderers find it difficult to use animals in design; they will rarely keep still long enough to be examined, photographed or drawn, their limbs are at different angles, they all have different heads, feet, tails, etc. You can rarely get away with drawing an animal badly; mistakes seem to be doubly obvious in this subject. *Don't despair*. There are other aspects of animal life which you may not have realized will make wonderful designs for embroidery, and after looking through the following pages you may find ideas which will entice you to try again.

8

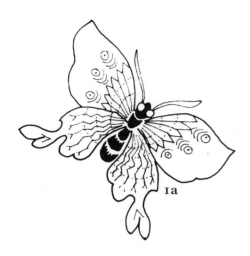

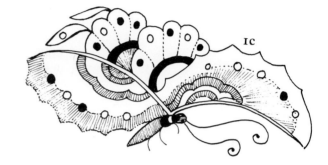

1a Butterfly, fifteenth-century Chinese woven silk
b A lace butterfly from Belgium; twentieth century
c Seventeenth-century Japanese butterfly embroidered in silk from a Nō robe

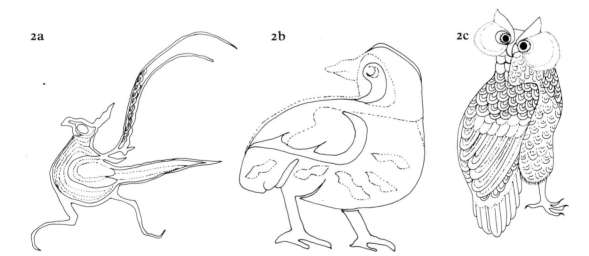

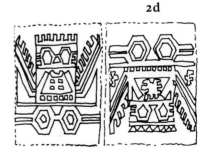

2a An embroidered bird found in an ancient grave in Pazyrik, Russia, showing considerable perception of the way the bird moves
b Nineteenth-century Chinese bird, embroidered with gold thread on silk
c Tapestry-woven bird from a Coptic garment
d An almost abstract interpretation of birds embroidered on a wool poncho, probably from the Paracas period of Peru, 500–400 BC

9

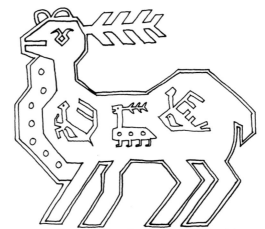

3 Reindeer from a Greek peasant embroidery.
Note the smaller creatures inside the body; this is
a feature of many embroideries of this type

4 Detail from a Sicilian quilt of the fourteenth
century, depicting part of the story of Tristram

5 A lion from one of the bed-curtains
embroidered by Abigail Pett in
seventeenth-century England

6 Part of a woven fragment from Tiahuanaco,
Peru, showing a monster, and probably dating
from the sixteenth century

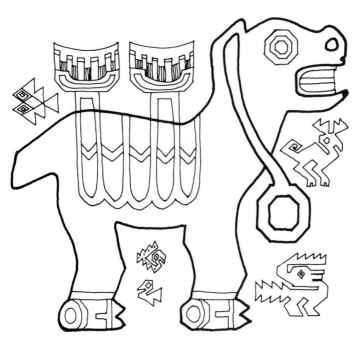

7 Part of an embroidered
hanging from west India;
twentieth century

8 Detail from the Bayeux Tapestry showing Duke
William on the black horse, wearing what may be
a quilted tunic, with two of his armoured
knights behind. Harold rides on in front during
a military expedition to defeat Count Conan of
Brittany

Sources of Design

1 *Observation* of animal life at first hand is, of course, essential to the study of potential design material. It is one's own personal knowledge of the subject which adds an extra dimension to a design, a reaction to the real thing which no photograph, drawing or sculpture can convey. It is unfortunately true that we only have the chance in our lifetimes to see for ourselves a minute fraction of the animal world and therefore we are sometimes obliged to make do with pre-recorded ideas. This should not deter us, however, from looking with extra perception at those creatures living around us—insects, pets, birds, fish and zoo animals—to note their fur-patterns and textures, their characteristic movements, eyes, paws and hoofs, horns and tails, fish scales and feathers, joints and all the other details which help to express the beauty of each creature. Look more closely at a police-horse, at the cows and horses standing in a field, at sheep, ladybirds, ducks and swans, hamsters and snails. Note their proportions, colours, shapes and anything else which catches your eye, and if possible, photograph or draw them.

The effect of drawing what you see is merely a form of visual note-taking, a way of helping you to remember, not for anyone else to see nor intended as a work of art. A quick sketch is all you need to note a leg joint or a foot. Not only will it remind you in the future, but the very act of sketching something plants it more firmly in the memory, just as writing down a poem does.

Using a camera is also an excellent way of recording what you see, especially as animals tend to move off just as you have whisked out a sketch pad and pencil.

2 *Books*. Useful design material may also be found in good wildlife books, but beware of painted pictures in some animal books as these are not always as accurate as they should be. The main drawback to this method is that the animal cannot be seen from every angle, so you can only use the shape as you see it in the picture.

Look out for old editions of the *National Geographic Magazine* which have wonderful photographs of the undersea world in them, rich in colour and texture, showing corals and exotic marine life.

3 *Museums* are a rich source of ideas, particularly as animal life has been well used on jewellery, pottery, glass, metalwork, woodwork, sculpture and

textiles. These animals will inevitably have been adapted by each craftsman, not only to suit his personal style but also according to the function of the artefact on which the decoration is placed and the material from which it is made. These factors play a decisive part in the form of the design; in the same way, the embroiderer adapts the style of her design according to the technique.

4 *Natural history museums* are excellent places for study as the creatures seen here are often difficult or impossible to see elsewhere. Sea-creatures, fossils and beautiful butterflies, exotic birds of paradise and skeletons of dinosaurs are there to be studied at leisure, from every angle.

9 Head of a sleeping tiger at the zoo

10 Watch horses in a field and make notes of details like ears and eyes, feathery legs, hooves, and areas of muscle showing through the coats. (*By courtesy of the Institute of Agricultural History and Museum of English Rural Life, University of Reading*)

11 When creatures move about constantly, a photograph will help your memory

12 Two snails:

a A Japanese wooden netsuke of the early
nineteenth century

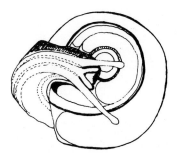

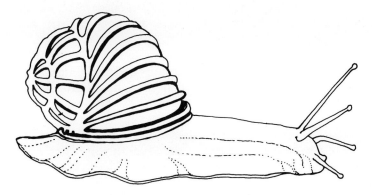

b A lamp in the form of a snail, by Chapelle and Muller, *c.* 1900

Collecting Material

Collect as many different kinds of reference material on one subject as you can—photographs, postcards, sketches, cuttings, pieces of fabric and threads, anything which sparks off an idea.

One special aspect of a subject may particularly appeal to you rather than a complete animal, for example patterns on skins and furs, butterflies' wings or horns and antlers. If this is the case, collect as much information as possible about the chosen subject, then:

1 Experiment with different embroidery techniques to find out ways of translating the subject. Keep these as samples.

2 Study the subject in depth over a period of time before you begin work on a series of projects directly related to it.

It is a good idea to keep all your reference material to do with one subject together in a folder, large envelope, scrap-book, or mounted on a folding display card. This will help you to clarify your ideas, prevent any pieces from going astray and will show at a glance what material you do or do not have.

13 Experiment by Jill Plumridge based on zebra stripes

14 Patterns on animals' faces are infinitely variable and make good subjects for detailed study and experiments

Types of Design

The first steps towards creating a design will depend on various factors, such as the embroidery technique you want to use and the article you wish to embroider.

Many people prefer their embroidery designs to be recognizable, actually to look like something identifiable and to have the correct colours—in other words, less of a design and more of a picture. This style is known as *realistic, naturalistic* or *representational*.

Some prefer their subject to be recognizable but slightly unreal, more decorative, perhaps using different colours and a more fanciful treatment in embroidery with a two-dimensional style. This may be called *stylized*, or *decorative*.

The removal of unnecessary details may so simplify a design as to render it *symbolic*. It may still be recognizable, although by this time it has been reduced to mere geometric shapes and lines which convey the basic image to those who see it.

Many designers work totally in the *abstract*, taking a basic idea from a drawing or sometimes a photograph, and changing its structure in various ways to create a pure design or pattern which can be used in embroidery. The end product may be totally unlike the original idea but this does not matter if it is pleasing to the eye.

There are various stages between these definitions, and many ways of interpreting them according to the artist. You will have to choose the style which suits you best according to your needs and personal preferences, and then steer more towards that one than towards the others.

15 Types of design:
a Realistic, naturalistic or representational. This shows the fish drawn exactly as it is seen, with nothing added or removed. It is meant to look exactly like a fish

20

b Stylized, or decorative. This is also meant to look like a fish, but not as exactly as the first design. The shape has been rounded and various details have been either exaggerated or left out, to suit the design

c Symbolic. The fish has now been reduced to three basic shapes. This is the simplest way in which it could be represented and still be recognizable.

d Abstract. An abstract design may or may not be recognized as the source from which it was derived. It is now purely design and hardly a fish at all

Each of these styles overlaps the other somewhat, and there are various stages between these definitions; there are also many different ways of interpreting them, according to the artist

16 These simple applied shapes of fabric are still recognizable as animals, though symbolic in style. Note the use of patterned fabric to help add some of the missing details. (*Photo: Gail Bathgate*)

17 OPPOSITE Shapes to make an elephant. Place a piece of tracing paper over a clear picture of an animal, preferably a fairly bulky one, and break it down into a series of geometric shapes. This type of design can be treated in a variety of ways, such as appliqué, padding and quilting, stitchery, pulled work and canvaswork

Designs to Fit Shapes

Another factor which affects the choice of design is the shape of the area to be filled. It may be a chair cover, a bag, a waistcoat or a box-top. In any case, shape and size will be important to you as some people work only on a large scale, and some the opposite. Your technique will also help to decide the shape.

Being fairly adaptable sources of design, many creatures can be made to fit into a variety of geometric shapes; some are by nature these shapes already! To find out what creatures fit which shapes best, cut different-shaped holes in pieces of paper and capture an animal picture inside the window. Much depends on the position of the animal, particularly in the case of larger creatures with long limbs. With fish and birds, the fins, tails and wings can easily be extended to fill in any spaces. Cats and some other small mammals look equally well sitting upright or lying down, and so are quite versatile. Snakes will fit any shape!

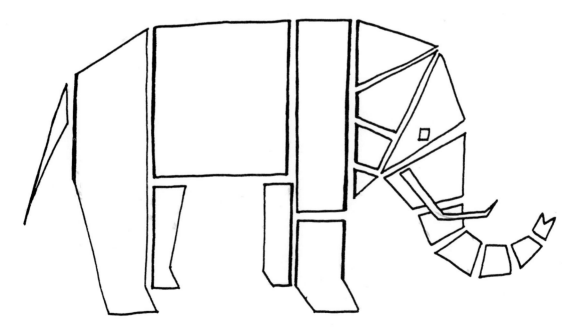

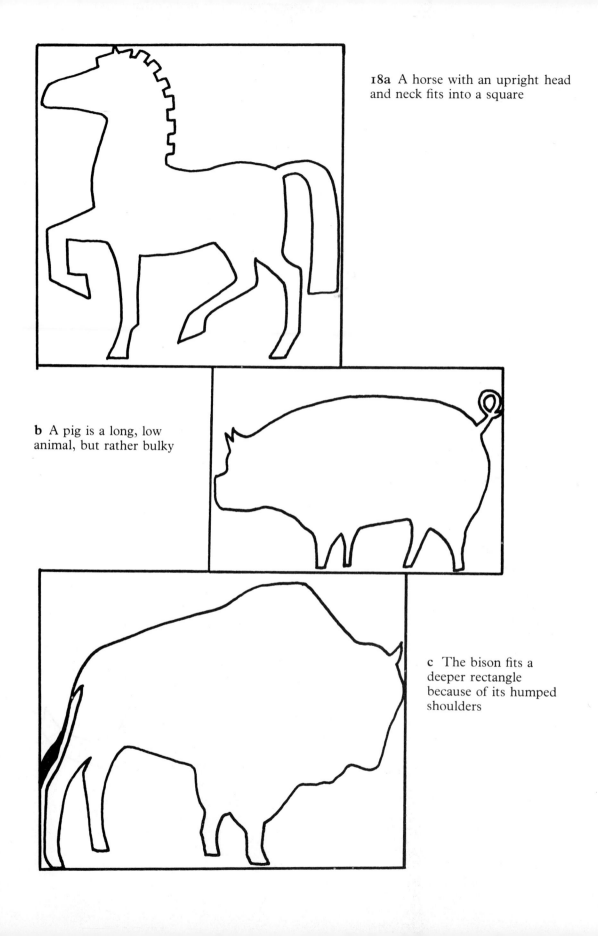

18a A horse with an upright head and neck fits into a square

b A pig is a long, low animal, but rather bulky

c The bison fits a deeper rectangle because of its humped shoulders

1 'Fantastic Beast', by Lady Hamilton Fairley. Canvaswork

2 'Laughing Boy', a three-dimensional tortoise by Anne Dyer. 23 cm (9 in.) long, made of felt and embroidered with raffene on sacking

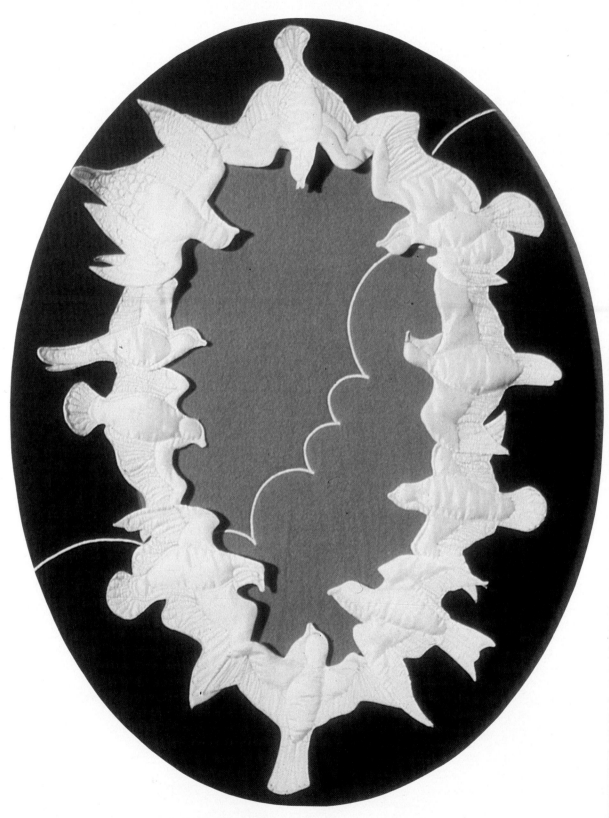

3 'Feather Boa', by Heather Durrough. The quilted, detachable birds in flight can also be worn as a collar. *(Photo: Heather Durrough)*

19 An almost abstract snake, decorated with areas of flat pattern, fits easily into a circle

20 An animal may be allowed to overflow its shape, like this squirrel. The inside of the triangle may be a different colour from the rest of the ground, to contrast with the fur colour, or it may be patterned fabric or stitch textures

21 OPPOSITE Some ways in which simplified animal shapes can be used on a quilt, a mobile, a folding book, a box and two cushions

Looking for Pattern

If a unit of design (or 'motif') is repeated often enough it becomes a pattern, no matter in what order or size it occurs. Feathers on a bird's wings, back and tail create a pattern; so do fish scales, zebra stripes, leopard spots and snake marks. These are some of the obvious examples; there are others where the pattern, because it is raised up from the surface, also creates a texture. The two should not be confused.

Animal patterns are great sources of inspiration to those looking for ideas for patchwork, canvaswork, quilting, pulled work and techniques where blocks of colour and/or stitching form the basis of the design.

22 Short, downy feathers already show signs of developing pattern in stripes, spots, patches and chevrons

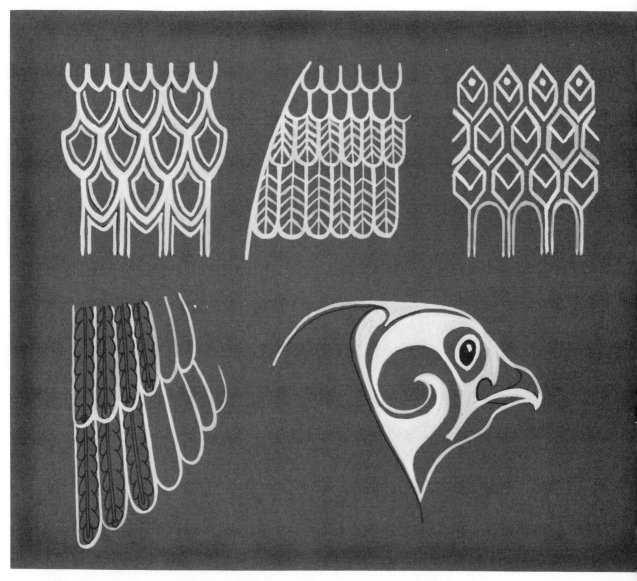

23 Feather patterns taken from carved reliefs of Ancient Egypt show a variety of formations. The falcon's head is also from the same source

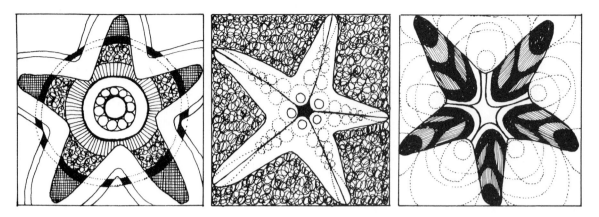

24 Starfish are easy shapes to repeat and so adapt well to pattern making. The three at the top show the same motif treated in different ways. The large detail shows the centre of a sea-urchin

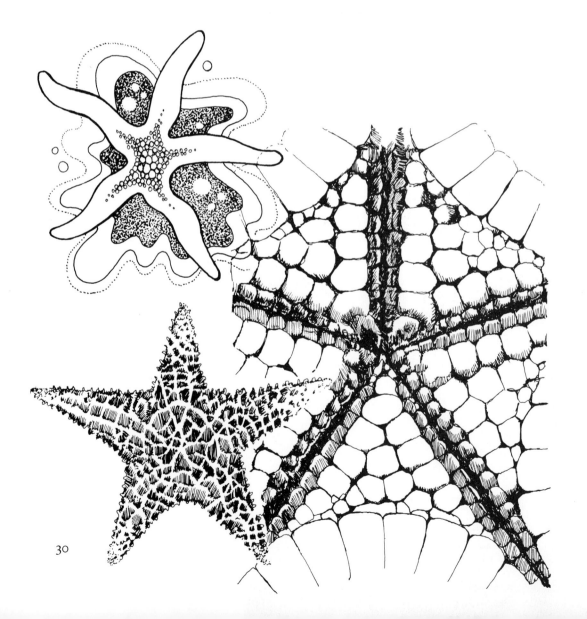

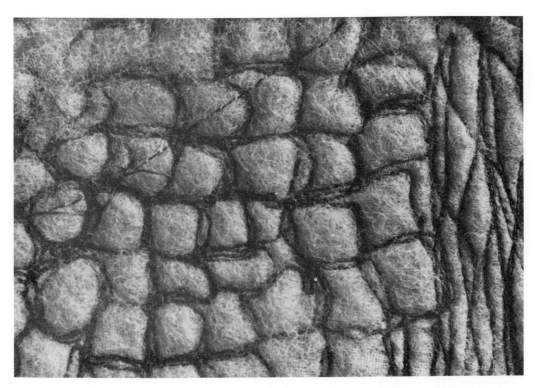

25 These two experiments reproduce exactly the pattern of the sea-urchin and the starfish seen in the drawing
a ABOVE Machine quilting by Paula Templeman
b Padding and ruched velvet. Small padded shapes are attached by hand stitching. By Anne Sutton

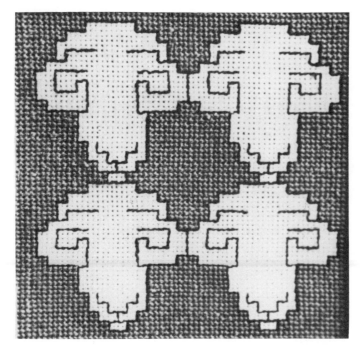

26 A pattern of rams' heads seen as Assisi work by Clare Emery. This method uses cross stitch to cover the background, leaving the motif void

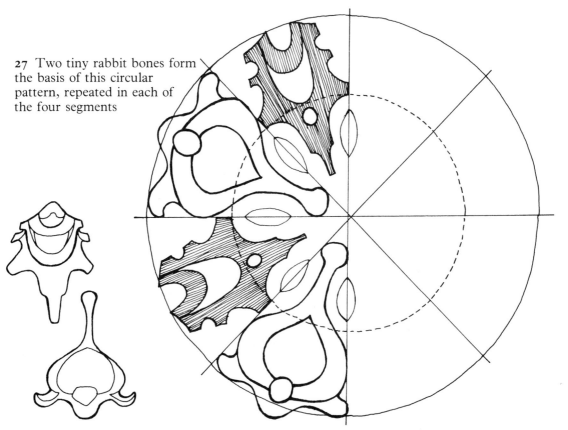

27 Two tiny rabbit bones form the basis of this circular pattern, repeated in each of the four segments

32

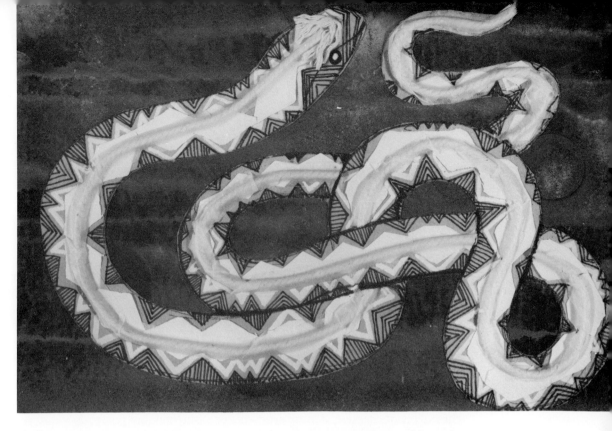

28 Cut paper, string and felt pens were used to create a pattern on this snake
which was then cut out and stuck on a roughly painted background

29 Pattern from the back of a tortoise

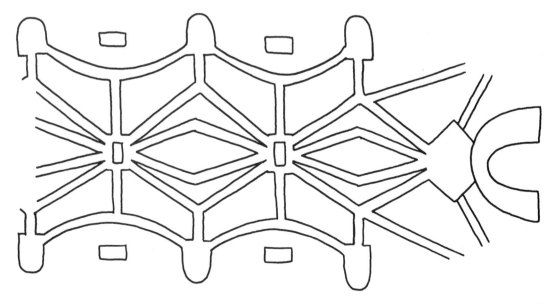

Colour

The use of colour in animal embroidery relates directly to the section on Types of Design as the colours you choose will depend almost entirely on whether your design is to be realistic or not. The 'picture' embroidery, where creatures are depicted as near life-like as possible, will require you to use colours near to the real ones. If you are to embroider a design based on your pet, you would still be likely to keep to the correct colours so that the animal would be identifiable, even though the style is not too realistic. In short, whether you keep to the natural colours or invent ones of your own depends on how far you wish to depart from realism and move towards the purely decorative. A pink crocodile or a blue dog are perfectly valid, not only to small children but also to designers using a scheme of colours which have been carefully chosen. Go ahead and use any colours you wish, but remember that some colours suggest movement, rage and ferocity while others suggest peace and calm. Therefore a ferocious-looking pink lion would not have quite the same impact as one in red or burnt-orange, neither would a dove of violent puce or black and white stripes convey the message usually associated with that bird.

The question of colour is also one of observation, to see where on the body the denser areas of colour are. Many creatures are paler underneath than on top, some have paler legs, butterflies' wings are duller underneath, and so on. The tonal areas are rarely the same all over.

Make use of the natural camouflage of many creatures; this is an interesting way of using only the parts of the animal which can be seen against its background and leaving the rest unseen.

30 Fallow deer are almost hidden as their spotted coats blend with the mottled background of sunlit foliage. This camouflage effect may be used in design

The Background: Animal Associations

In the following chapters dealing with the various types of animals, I have included lists of 'associations' in the hope that these will help to formulate a complete design idea, rather than one using an animal alone.

In our minds, many creatures seem to fit naturally into a particular role, for example: March hare, cat and mouse, sheepdog and sheep, tiger and cage, horse and circus, doves and dovecote, shells and rocky pool. There are many of these mental associations, varying from person to person, which often help to make a design meaningful.

Kittens in flower pots and puppies in wellington boots, however, have had their day, and belong now to the realms of 'tapestry packs'. Complete beginners in embroidery should never feel that they must begin with poor design.

Nevertheless, there is no reason at all why one *must* have a background of any kind in a design based on animal life. If the creature is decorative enough by means of its shape and treatment a background may be quite unnecessary; it is for you, the designer, to decide.

31 Delicate embroideries with no backgrounds may be mounted as a set of two, three or four. Butterflies and other small creatures look particularly well in this way

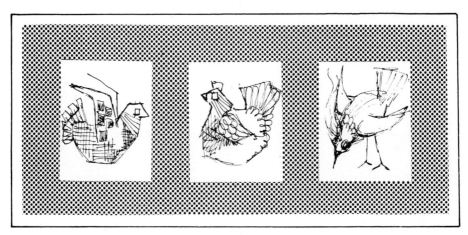

32 'Butcher's Shop' by Barbara Hirst. This may be, to some, a grisly association with animal life, but the interpretation shows good attention to detail without being fussy, and a quiet humour in its treatment

33 This magnificent lion faces an identical one on the other side of the steps of a public building in Norwich. The patterned background of plinth, windows, stonework and balconies is a perfect foil to the animal's sinuous lines and would need only a little adaptation to render it almost abstract. Note that the association of lion and sculpture emphasizes the heraldic nature of the subject

37

Some Ways of Presenting a Design

34 Animal shapes may sometimes be superimposed for fun to make a composite or 'ghost' design. These two fit well, resulting in two rather bewildered expressions

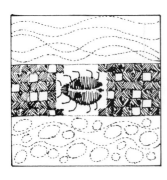

35a TOP: quilted lines
CENTRE: canvaswork
BOTTOM: quilted pebbles

b Appliqué or goldwork shell with couched or quilted lines

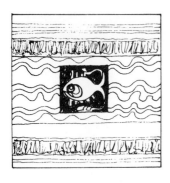

c Piped and pin-tucked lines and frayed fabric top and bottom. Stitched fish with couched ripples

d Blackwork bison with three lines of wrapped card. (i.e. card strips wrapped with black, white, grey and gold threads)

e Tiny appliqué animals between two strips of canvaswork. The strip at the base should be of a deeper tone

f Bird framed by window, set slightly off centre

g Pulled work cat framed by padded stonework

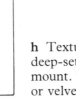

h Textural fish and coral, deep-set into padded circular mount. The mount could be calico or velvet

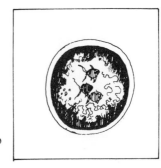

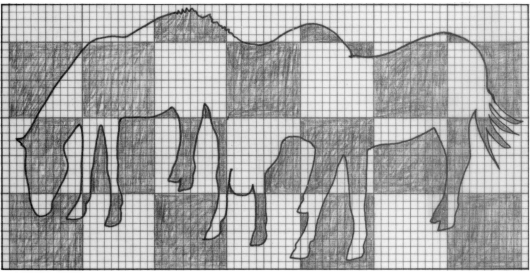

37 Cows in the home pasture seen on three planes, the foreground, middle-distance and distance. To accentuate this, the photograph has been cut into five unequal strips and replaced in such a way as to draw more attention to the nearest cow. This design may be interpreted in several ways, one of which might be to use a more textural technique on one or two of the nearer panels and a lighter technique on the other three. To keep some element of continuity, one would introduce a little of each technique into all five panels

36a OPPOSITE Przewalski's horses, natives of Mongolia, make an interesting group with the contrasting tones of manes, tails and legs
b The outline of the group has been traced onto graph paper and the chequered pattern superimposed, except that where the design overlaps this, the black and white is reversed. This idea could be the basis of a design for patchwork

Fantastic Beasts

ANIMALS IN HERALDRY

The system of heraldry was devised in the Middle Ages when men went into battle covered from head to toe in armour, thus disguising their identity. In order to differentiate between the various combatants, coloured devices were painted on the shields and embroidered on tunics, banners and horse trappings. These devices always had some significance peculiar to that person or family and had to be quickly and easily recognizable; they were therefore often highly stylized, sometimes merely symbolic.

Although heraldic embroidery was usually done by professionals, the young women of the house would also embroider heraldic animals on their samplers for future use on household linen.

Coats of arms were not only shown on the family possessions but on articles owned by the guilds and livery companies. Banners, servants' livery, badges and other accessories were made of the most sumptuous and glittering materials to display the prosperity of the brotherhood.

Designs were often suggested by modifying the family name to sound similar to that of a bird or animal, by making a pun on the name, or by using an animal whose qualities emphasized the family motto. Among animals most often seen in the earliest heraldic embroideries are the lion, the unicorn, the dragon and the stag. Birds were also common, particularly the swan, the falcon, the eagle and the swallow (referred to in heraldry as the martlet). Sometimes a coat of arms was derived from a symbol rooted in ancient history. For example, the White Horse of Kent and Hanover was originally a Saxon totem animal, the Dragon of Wales was a Roman ensign, and the Eagle of the Holy Roman Empire was originally the Eagle of Jupiter, also used on the battle standards of the Roman legions.

Today, heraldic embroidery is a highly specialized craft, for not only must the work itself be of a very high standard but the design must be accurate in every detail and conform to the rules of heraldry, of which there are many. The positions of animals on the design are of great importance, as are the exact colours. The design as a whole should, of course, fit the area for which it is intended. Before work of this nature is undertaken, it is essential to ensure that every detail of the design is correct.

FANTASTIC BEASTS

The *lion*, sometimes termed a 'leopard', is the symbol of courage and power, generally seen either standing upright waving his legs in the air (rampant), or walking (passant).

The *unicorn* is a mythical beast of very ancient origin, particularly popular in the Middle Ages in Europe. It has the body of a sleek white horse, the hooves of an antelope (cloven hooves), a lion's tail and a goat's beard. It has a single twisted horn from the forehead, four feet long with a white base, black centre and red tip. The only person able to tame this fierce beast is a young maiden wearing a garland of flowers. The lion and

38 Heraldic emblems were embroidered on a soldier's equipment in order to identify him on the battlefield

the unicorn were rivals for the title 'King of Beasts', and the latter may sometimes be seen wearing a crown around his neck.

The *centaur* has the trunk of a man on a horse's body and legs. Derived from early Greek mythology, he was probably created when men on horseback from the north were mistakenly thought to be combined creatures. Sagittarius (the archer) is the best known centaur, now the ninth sign of the zodiac. He was originally the wise and immortal Chiron who was accidentally wounded by Hercules. Chiron was renowned for his knowledge of music, medicine and archery.

Pegasus, a true horse with great wings, was reputed to be one of the kindest creatures in mythology. He was also regarded as the horse of the Muses.

Dragons are known in almost every country of the world. The Eastern Dragon is the most important creature in oriental traditions. Different dragons have different functions to care for the natural order of things, and while these powerful creatures are often quite kindly they can also be temperamental. One such creature is the Chinese Dragon who presides over the eastern quadrant of the compass and represents Royalty, Rain and Spring.

By comparison, the Western Dragon is utterly evil, being the symbol of strength and power. It was adopted as a warlike emblem by ancient peoples and carved by the Vikings on the prows of their ships and on their shields. Descriptions vary: it may be almost any colour, its scaly body shines brilliantly, smoke and fire issue from its nostrils, and its broad wings are set vertically on its shoulders.

The Welsh Dragon (Y Ddraig Goch) is always red, and has a shorter, more upright stance than other dragons. The tail is narrow and the wings are usually shown extended.

The *Phoenix* is a mythical Egyptian bird with feathers of red and gold and rainbow-coloured wings. The eyes are sea-blue, the feet purple, and its plumage shimmers and glows when it flies. According to legend the Phoenix lived in a sacred wood in Paradise, and when it neared the end of its thousand-year lifespan flew away westwards to Phoenicia, picking up precious spices in Arabia on the way. It made its new nest from the spices but the sun accidentally set fire to it and the bird was destroyed. Immediately, a new Phoenix began to grow from the ashes, and as soon as it was strong enough, the new bird placed the ashes on the altar of the Sun Temple in Egypt before flying on to Paradise for the next thousand years. The Phoenix represents Resurrection, Beauty, Goodness, Warmth, Prosperity, Peace and the Sun, as well as other attributes.

A *Mermaid* has the top half of a beautiful woman and the lower half of a fish. Her long hair (which she combs when a storm is brewing) is sometimes green, sometimes golden. She is seen in medieval heraldry, on mosaic floors, stone and wood carving, ships' figure-heads and on inn signs. She was known, as were mermen, as far back as Babylonian times and in very many countries of the world.

The *Yale*, one of the Queen's Beasts, was first portrayed on the arms of

John Beaufort, Duke of Somerset in 1440. It resembles an antelope, but has the head and body of a horse, a goat's beard and large upright tusks. Its body is hairy and spotted, with a tufted tail, and cloven hooves like an antelope. Its large curved horns can swivel in any direction to assist in fighting.

ANIMALS IN CHRISTIAN SYMBOLISM

Many animals have been used to symbolize the various aspects of Christian life and teaching, as they also have for other religions. As animals used in this way are also represented in later chapters, only the ones which are traditionally treated rather differently are shown here.

Some of the best-known are:

The *Phoenix*, often used to symbolize the Resurrection.

The *Pelican*, symbolizing the sacrifice on the cross and the Holy Communion.

The *Unicorn*, whose legend is often taken as an allegory of the Incarnation of Christ in the Virgin Mary.

The *Lamb*, a well-known symbol of Christ. The Agnus Dei or Lamb of God indicates Christ carrying the Banner of Victory.

The *Dove*, a symbol of the Holy Spirit. Seven doves represent the seven gifts of the Holy Spirit. When it carries an olive branch it represents peace and forgiveness.

The *Fish*, the earliest sign used by Christians. The sign of three fishes is often used to represent the Trinity, as are three hares.

The *Lion*, the symbol of strength, the tribe of Judah, and also of Christ.

The *Sheep*, symbolizing God's pastoral care for man, in both Old and New Testaments.

The *Cockerel*, a symbol of the Passion and also St Peter's emblem.

39 The Pella Lion, by Maureen Rendell. A design based on pebble mosaics from Pella, Macedonia. Blackwork on white silk coloured with Pentel dye-sticks

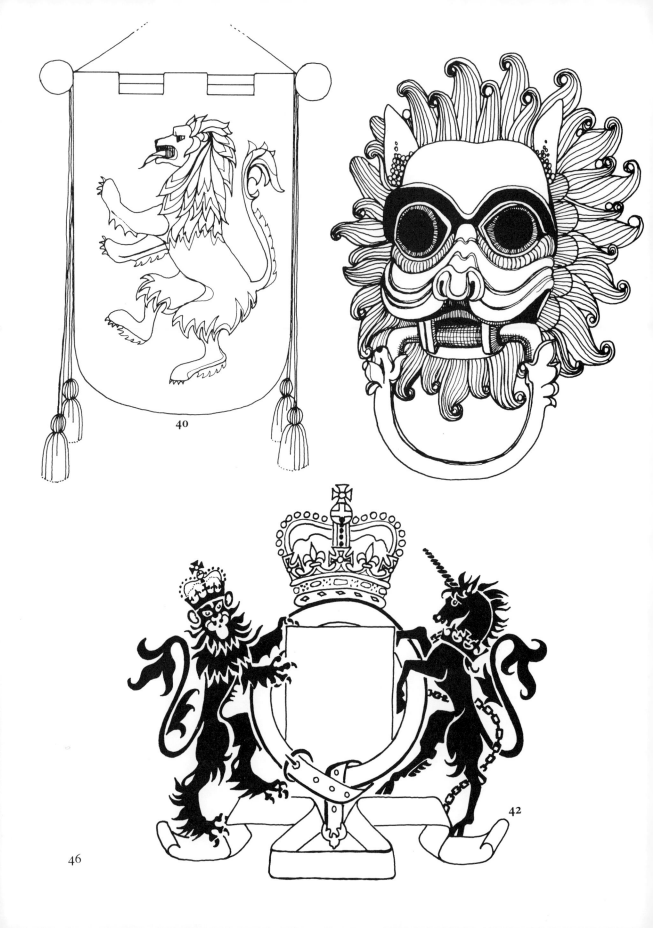

40

42

46

43 Unicorn. A gentle, mystical creature such as this calls for a soft and subtle colour-scheme of white, greys, silver and gold, pinks, mauves and blues

OPPOSITE

40 A banner with a heraldic motif, such as this lion, makes a colourful wall-hanging worked in appliqué, canvaswork or heavy stitchery

41 The lion's head sanctuary door knocker from Durham Cathedral would make a splendid three-dimensional piece in padded felts and leather

42 The lion and the unicorn here act as supporters to the shield

44 Centaur

45 Pegasus

4 'Eastern Dragon', by Jan Messent. Canvaswork

5 'Geranuk', by Jean Parry. Canvaswork and free stitchery on a soft canvas, leaving the background uncovered

46 A chinese festival dragon seen at the Commonwealth Institute in London. The extravagantly be-whiskered head, the beard and gaping mouth, and the brilliantly scaled body would make a perfect design for embroidery. (*Photo: V. A. Campbell-Harding*)

47 Design of an Eastern Dragon for canvaswork

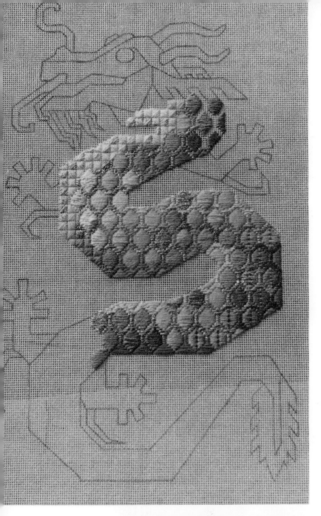

48a Partly worked canvas embroidery of the Eastern Dragon design. Single canvas, 14s, with the design drawn on in fine felt pen

b The head of the Eastern Dragon showing a detail of the stitches used

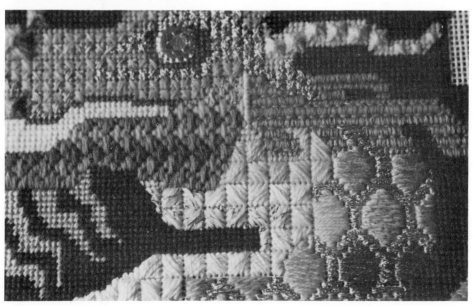

50 Welsh Dragon

49 OPPOSITE Western Dragon; a painting made for the sixth birthday of the author's first son

51 Phoenix. This design is open to a variety of interpretations but should, I think, reflect the drama which the story implies: fierce heat, tragic death, movement, perhaps panic and then re-birth. The background should be kept simple as a foil to the activity of the motif

52 OPPOSITE Mermaid. Inset is a Celtic carving of a merman from a stone at Meigle in Perthshire, Scotland

53 Two of the Queen's Beasts, the Yale of the Beauforts and the White Horse (Unicorn) of Kent and Hanover

54 Cross stitch interpretations of a crowned leopard, or lion, and the hanging fleece. The fleece symbol can be seen on the coat of arms of several towns and cities, denoting the wool spinning or weaving industries

55 'Bacon Banner', by Anne Dyer. 'A pig rampant on a field of grass'
throws a new light on the traditional heraldic use of words. This banner was
made for a Californian policeman of the embroiderer's aquaintance, a
member of a narcotics squad whose surname was Bacon. (*Photo: A. Dyer*)

56 An interwined design of two beasts taken from
the *Book of Kells* (Middle sixth to early seventh
century). This type of zoomorphic design is
typical of Celtic work to be seen on manuscripts
and stone carvings in many parts of the British
Isles. Enlarged, it could be quilted onto the back
of a jacket or waistcoat, and also on a matching
bag. The square format also makes it ideal for
decorating a cushion-cover or a set of matching
chair seats

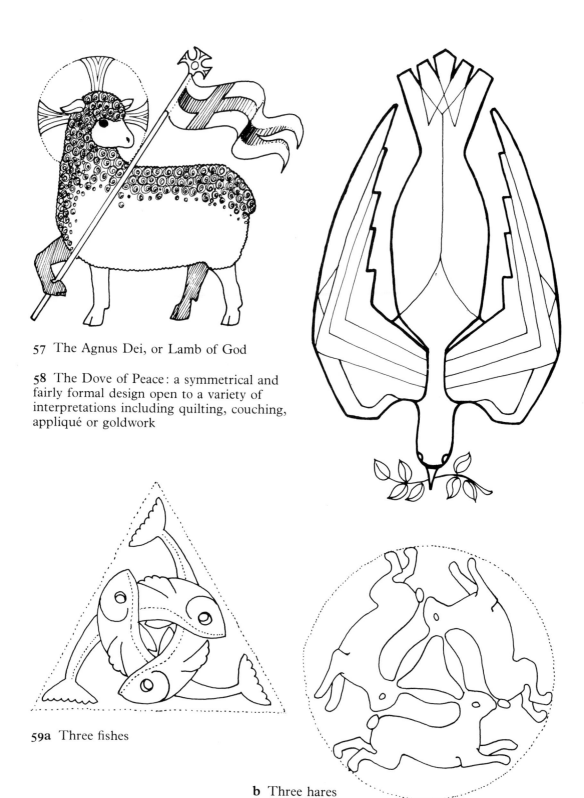

57 The Agnus Dei, or Lamb of God

58 The Dove of Peace: a symmetrical and fairly formal design open to a variety of interpretations including quilting, couching, appliqué or goldwork

59a Three fishes

b Three hares

Tiny Creatures

The uncomplicated, symmetrical and varied shapes of invertebrates make them ideal subjects for embroidery, although only a very small proportion of them are represented here as examples of the most decorative species.

Unlike mammals, butterflies do not need to be identified as being of any particular species, making the pleasure of designing according to whim so much fun. However, it is still essential to look closely at a good photograph or biological drawing to note the head and two body sections, to see where the wings are attached and to identify the correct number of legs and other anatomical details. Although details can be adapted for the sake of embroidery, it is when dealing with unfamiliar anatomies that mistakes can occur which spoil the credibility of the design.

When looked at objectively many tiny creatures are seen to be extremely beautiful and probably deserve more attention than we give them. Their compact body shapes make beetles ideal for canvas and pulled-thread work, and metal-thread embroidery is an excellent way of reproducing the sheen of the wing-cases and the fragile legs.

The Elizabethans were very fond of embroidering tiny creatures on their clothes, including caterpillars and snails, but today we have the advantage of a wider range of techniques for our interpretations. Place them in masses of highly textural foliage, on large moss-covered stones, on canvaswork tree barks, on boxes, *in* boxes, caterpillars on cabbage leaves and moths around a candle-flame.

ASSOCIATIONS
1 Bees and wasps: beehive, honeycomb, jars of honey, sewing bee, wasps' nest.
2 Worms: inch-worm, larva tunnels and galleries, tree bark, compost.
3 Beetles: beetle drive, Beatlemania, beetle-brows.
4 Snails: plate of snails, snail's pace, grub (food).

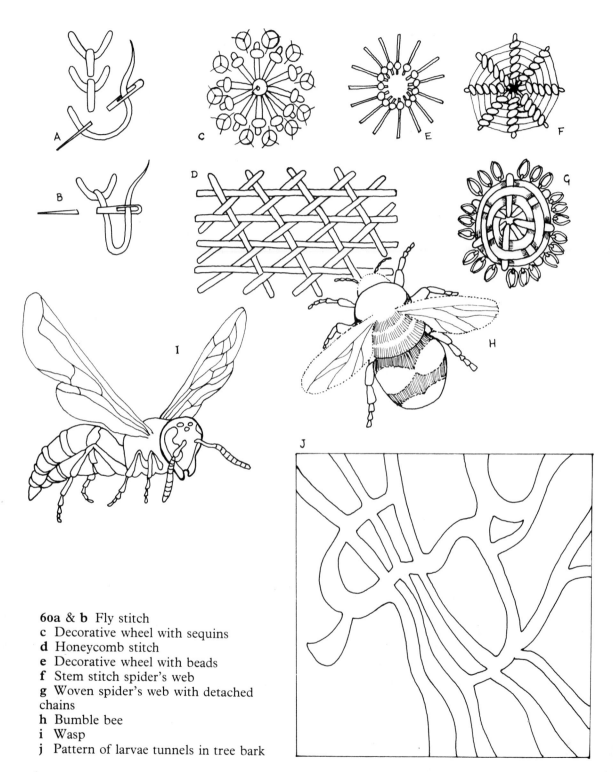

60a & **b** Fly stitch
c Decorative wheel with sequins
d Honeycomb stitch
e Decorative wheel with beads
f Stem stitch spider's web
g Woven spider's web with detached chains
h Bumble bee
i Wasp
j Pattern of larvae tunnels in tree bark

62

61

63

61 Canvaswork bee by Kit Pyman.
(*Photo: K. Pyman*)

62 Canvaswork beetle by Kit Pyman.
(*Photo: K. Pyman*)

63 Spider's web. Notice the curves of the radiating threads, heavy with beads of dew

64 Tunnels made by beetle larvae inside tree bark

64

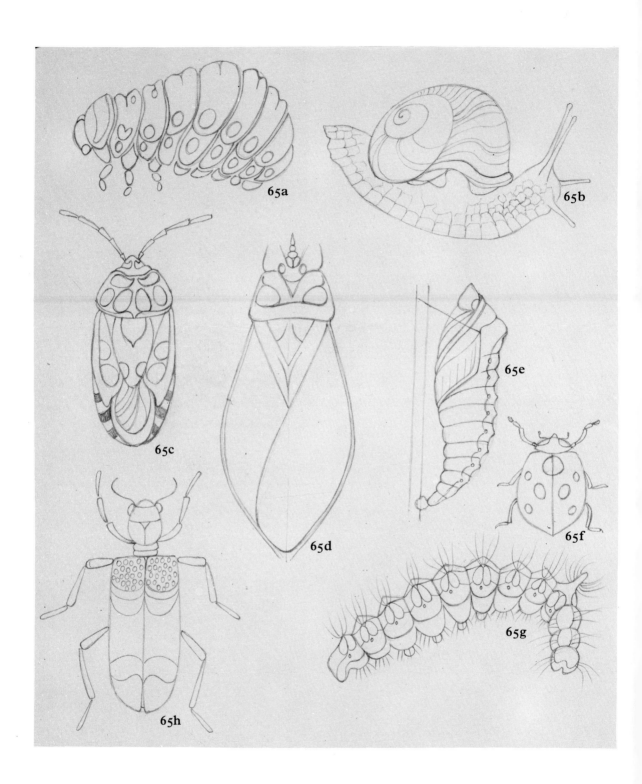

65a

65b

65c

65d

65e

65f

65g

65h

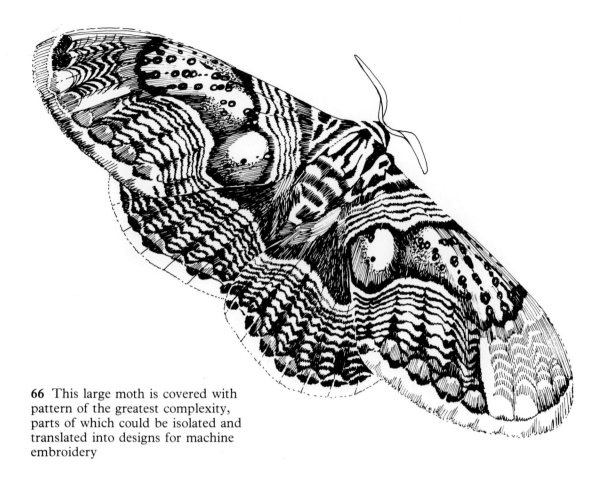

66 This large moth is covered with pattern of the greatest complexity, parts of which could be isolated and translated into designs for machine embroidery

65 OPPOSITE Drawings of beautiful little creatures, some rather simplified
a Larva of the Colorado Beetle
b Edible snail
c Shield bug
d Detail of water scorpion
e Chrysalis
f Ladybird
g Caterpillar
h Beetle (adapted)

69 A beaded and sequined butterfly used as a dress ornament. The use of beads, sequins, jewels and metal threads in the embroidery helps to convey the rich iridescence of the wings

OPPOSITE

67 Macramé butterfly by Kit Pyman, made of fine cord in half hitches and double hitches, and incorporating beads. (*Photo: K. Pyman*)

68 Casalguidi work by Clare Emery. A three-dimensional pulled-work butterfly approaches flowers in raised stitchery

65

70 Butterflies have many forms, some tiny and plain, some very large with bold and brilliant patterns. Features from several may be combined in one insect

Underwater Life

There is probably a wider range of design possibilities in this area of animal life than in any of the others, as nowhere else is there such a diversity of shape, size, colour, texture and pattern from which to choose. Because of the complexity of the subject, it is worthwhile examining the various structures under separate headings to discover their design potential and the ways in which they may be simplified and used.

MICROSCOPIC ORGANISMS

These are often based on simple geometric shapes. Many are circular, lending themselves easily to pattern-making and to single motifs for decorating items such as box tops, mats, clothes and cushions. Sometimes two or three simple shapes may be superimposed upon each other to create a more complex motif. Note the delicate transparency of these creatures and try to recreate this in the embroidery technique you use.

SEA ANEMONES, SEA URCHINS AND JELLYFISH

This is a very decorative group which may be used in many ways, for example, in delicate goldwork or shadow quilting, or perhaps in a highly textural technique suggested by thickly waving tentacles and spines. If the real thing is not available, it is essential to study diagrams and photographs of these underwater animals as their sometimes rough appearance belies their very organized construction. Note where and how the spines and tentacles are actually joined to the body, as this information may even add to the decorative value of the design. Use the semi-transparency of some creatures in this group as an extra dimension in your design, either by your choice of delicate nets and organzas or in gently sparkling threads and beads.

SHELLS

These range from highly complex structures to the very simplest shapes, and so may be used either whole or in part. The urge to 'do something' with a particularly beautiful shell may be frustrated time and again by its very complexity—all those twists and curls, ridges and coils! Examine the shell in parts instead of as a whole shape. Look at the pattern on its surface (either of colours or ridges or bumps) and make a note of this. Draw a very small area of the shell which has a particularly lovely curve to it. View it from all angles, making small unrelated sketches of its parts, then try to develop a few of these sketches as exercises in pattern or line. These may then be used at some future time in another context.

If the shell has a reasonably simple and interesting shape, then note *this* in a drawing instead of looking for other details. Make outline drawings of several shell shapes and try them as exercises in a variety of techniques, then develop the most successful of these as a design for a particular purpose.

STARFISH AND SHELLFISH

A certain amount of detailed observation is needed again here, as even a simple starfish may not be quite as simple as a first glance may suggest. They vary considerably in size, shape, number of arms, texture, pattern and colour. Some are almost limbless! Their shapes make them ideal for pattern-making, as they fit neatly into a circle or square. As single motifs they can be combined with pebbles, shells and seaweed, and will adapt quite easily to most embroidery techniques, particularly quilting, padding and appliqué. A three-dimensional, well padded starfish decorated with beads makes an attractive pin-cushion (if you can bear the idea) as also does a sea-urchin.

Shellfish include the rather more complicated lobsters and crabs in all their varieties. Claws need careful counting, and although a certain lee-way is allowed for design purposes it is always a good idea to note features such as joints, segments and tails to give your design credibility and consequently more interest. In fact, many extra design details are sure to emerge as a result of careful investigation. Exaggerate scalloped edges of shells and long, curving antennae, smooth out curves of claws and examine the undersides for beautifully arranged softer parts.

FISH

It is usually easier and more visually attractive to depict the profile of a fish rather than any other angle, thus eliminating problems of perspective in a design. However, the wide variety of these profiles is unfortunately seldom exploited to fullest advantage in design generally, not to mention the variety of patterns, colours and textures. Like shells, fish may be studied for their detail alone or for their overall shape. Observe them in aquaria in their natural surroundings, in museums of natural history where exotic ones are easier to draw, or freshly bought from a fishmonger where you can examine the construction in greater detail and make exact notes of eyes, gills, fins, scales and tail as well as the bone structure. This last method of research is an invaluable way of obtaining good design material. Look also at good book illustrations, particularly of tropical fish whose wonderful displays of colour, pattern and shape make excellent embroidery designs. Flashes of gold and silver, sparkling sequins and rich colours, enhance even the most ordinary fish shape, but differences can be achieved also by changing the position of the fins (those on the back and underneath) and the shape of the gills and tail. These details can be varied considerably, helping to suggest vitality and movement in your design.

ASSOCIATIONS

As underwater life is one of the most versatile design sources, the possible interpretations and techniques are almost limitless. Accompanying material for underwater subjects could include:

1 Rocks and pebbles, rock-pools and sea-shore.
2 Seaweeds and corals.
3 Ripples, waves, river-bed, waterfall, salmon-leap.
4 Nets, lobster-pots, fishing-rods and hooks.
5 Fish wrapped in paper, glass bowl, plate and basket, loaves and fishes, 'like a fish out of water', a fishy story.

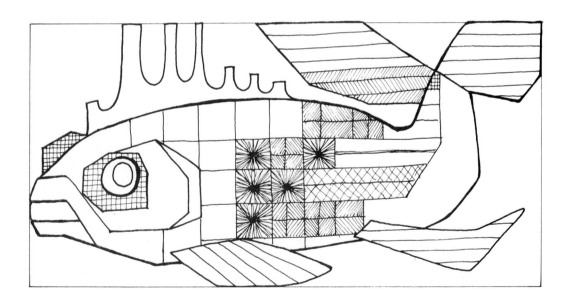

71 A canvaswork design which could also be used for pulled-work. Suitable for a box, cushion, or the book-cover of a fisherman's journal

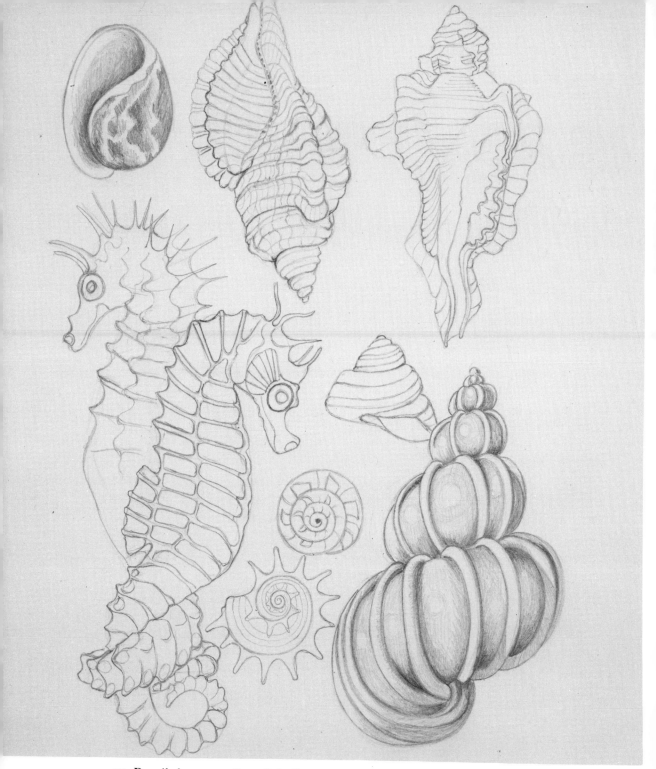

72 Pencil-drawn studies of shells and sea-horses are not only a means of recording what is seen but also an aid to observation. In this way one can become more aware of the wealth of design which would otherwise lie unnoticed

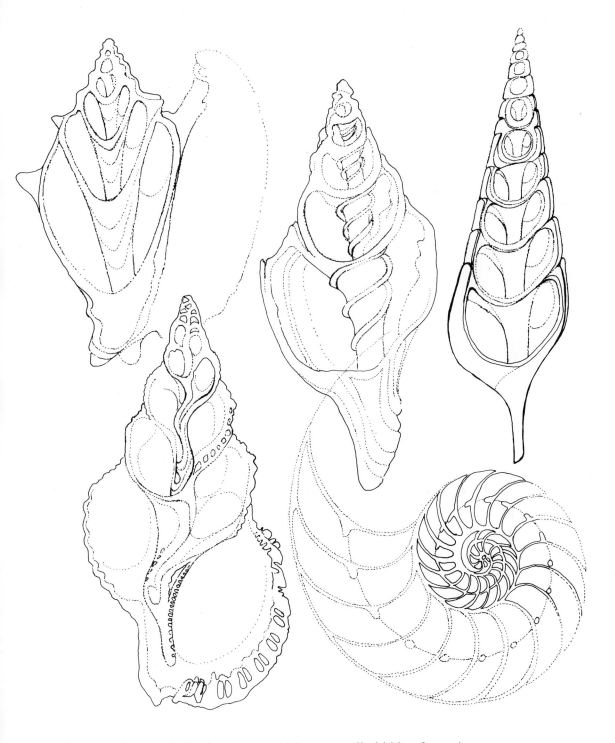

73 Cross-sections of shells show parts which are usually hidden from view.
A small part of any of these studies could be the basis of an exercise in
line or shape using threads and fabric. Use a paper window to isolate a
small area

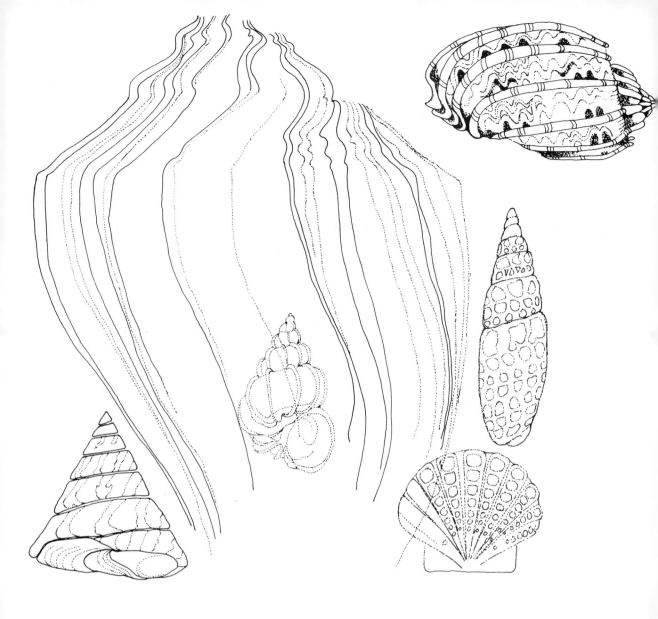

74 Studies of exterior shell decoration. The shapes of the shells vary greatly, as do the types of pattern on them, some in colours and some in textured ridges. Try to manipulate the fabric to create similar effects

75 OPPOSITE A light-hearted use of lettering combines happily in these two instances where the shapes of the letters actually help to define the parts of the bodies, especially the G on the fish and the B on the lobster

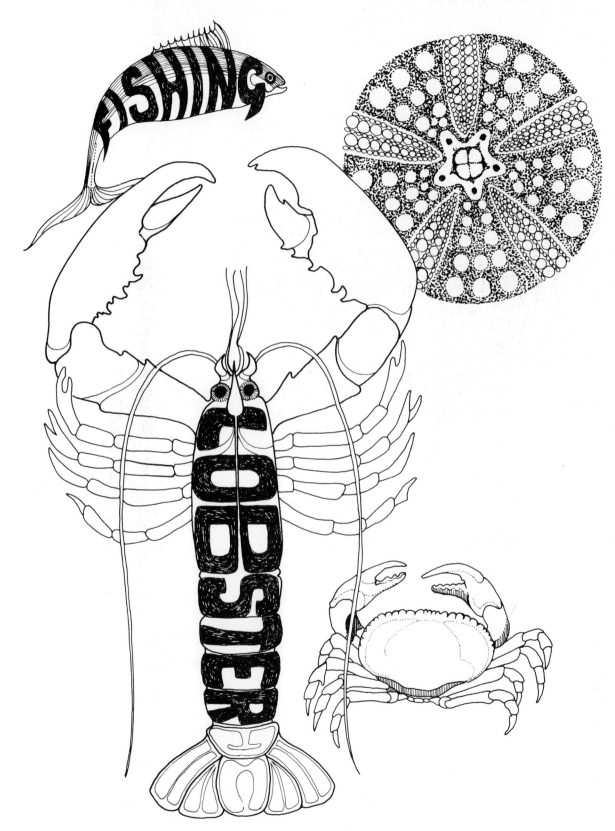

73

76a

76a Simple shells with beautifully smooth
curves suggest an equally simple
treatment
b Shadow quilting by Lyn Hughes. A
layer of shaped felt pieces is sandwiched
between sheer organdie and calico, and
hand-stitched round the edges

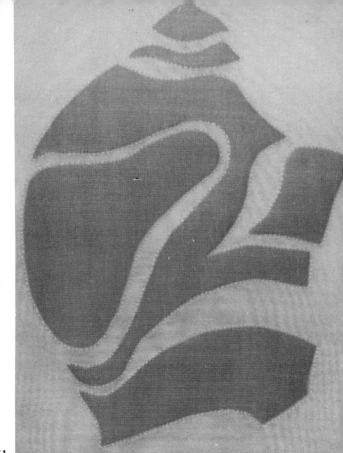

76b

77 Portuguese Man o' War jellyfish   77

78 An assortment of shells, sea-horses
and corals showing a variety of textures,
patterns and shapes

78

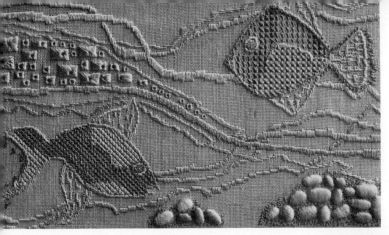

79 LEFT Pulled-work fish by Lyn Hughes, worked on an evenweave linen with a background of eyelet squares, lines of satin stitch and padded satin stitch pebbles. Threads of white and gold are used on a white fabric

80 RIGHT Fish, in Hardanger embroidery, by Lyn Hughes. This is a drawn-thread technique worked on a double-weave fabric using blocks of satin stitch. Some metal threads have been added for a glittering effect

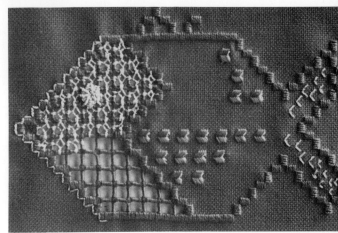

81 Fish within a fish. A fun interpretation, suitable perhaps for a hanging in a child's room. The small fish may be brightly coloured with added jewels, beads and metal threads, with the background colours of a darker or more neutral tone

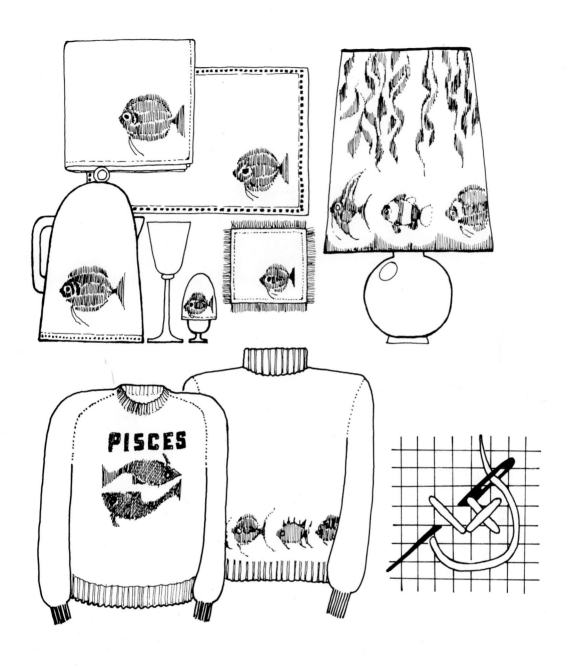

82a OPPOSITE Fish designs for cross stitch
b Some articles on which the cross-stitch fish may be worked. The stitch is usually worked over two threads in each direction as shown. The designs may also be knitted into sweaters, or embroidered on afterwards in Swiss darning

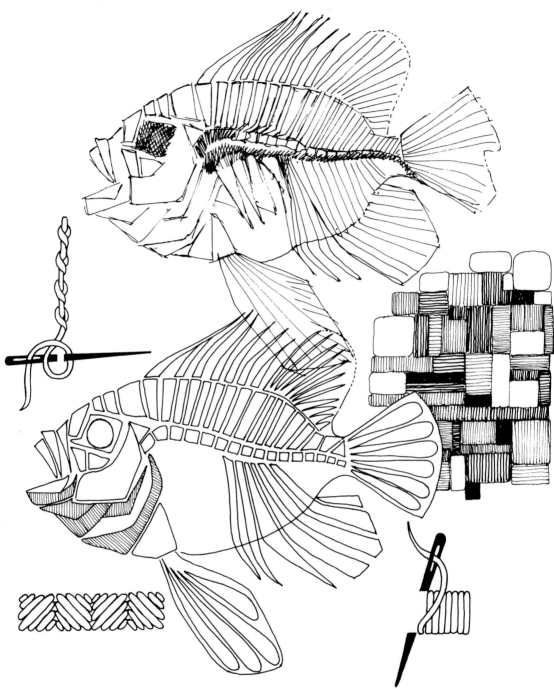

83 TOP: a rough sketch of a fossil fish showing the horny scale and bone parts of the body and tail

BELOW: translated into a more ordered design suitable for interpretation using blocks of stitches and a textured line such as coral stitch

Coral stitch is shown on the left (above), satin stitch on the right

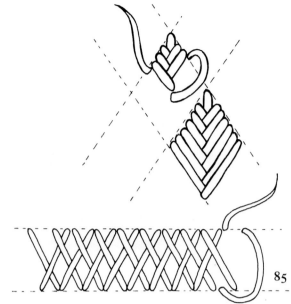

84

85

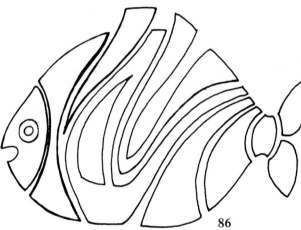

86

84 A swimming fish in decoratively swirling water shows how the background can imply action and mood. (*By courtesy of Dover Publications*)

85 TOP: fishbone stitch. Used in this formation it may suggest fish scales
BELOW: closed Herringbone stitch

86 Cut paper fish; a simple design useful for appliqué or goldwork

87 Two Puffer fish showing a similar pattern of lines running in the opposite direction

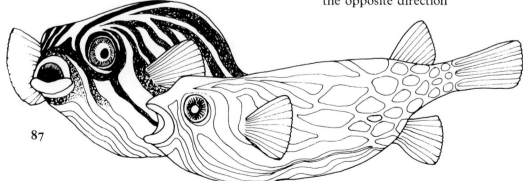

87

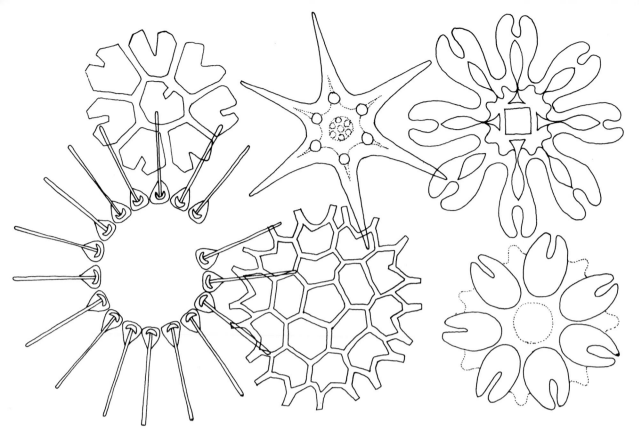

88a Microscopic organisms make
good isolated motifs for stitchery
or quilting.
b For more complex designs, two
of the above motifs have been
combined. Metal threads and
beads would add a richness to
these designs

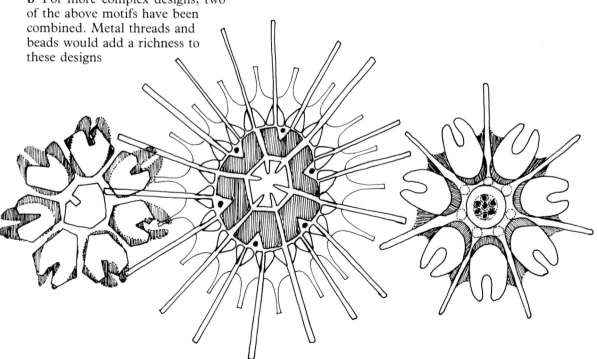

Amphibians and Reptiles

Although these creatures are not, to most people, the most appealing, they have much to offer the embroiderer in terms of design ideas. The variety of decorative and compact shapes, the sinuous bodies, the richly patterned and textured skins are perfect starting points for many kinds of experimentation in techniques. These could perhaps simulate the quilted effect of some lizard skins, the raised bumps of crocodiles (padding), the elaborate patterns of chameleons (machine embroidery), and the appliqué and patchwork effect of some snakeskins and tortoise shells. A little exploration will reveal that the possibilities are enormous.

ASSOCIATIONS
1 Frogs and toads: foliage, garden ponds, water, frog-spawn, mossy stones and pebbles, water-lilies, the frog-prince fairy tale.
2 Lizards, geckos and chameleons: moss and lichen-covered stones, sand, large leaves, tree-bark and branches, part changes of colour.
3 Crocodiles: water (part in, part out), sandy banks and grasses, crocodile tears, handbags and shoes.
4 Turtles, tortoises and terrapins: in water or on sandy beach, boulders, foliage, hibernation box, turtle soup!
5 Snakes: trees, water, foliage, sand, rocks, snake-charmer and basket.

89 Chameleon. The tail is a decorative feature which can curl around the design or be used to help the balance wherever a space needs filling

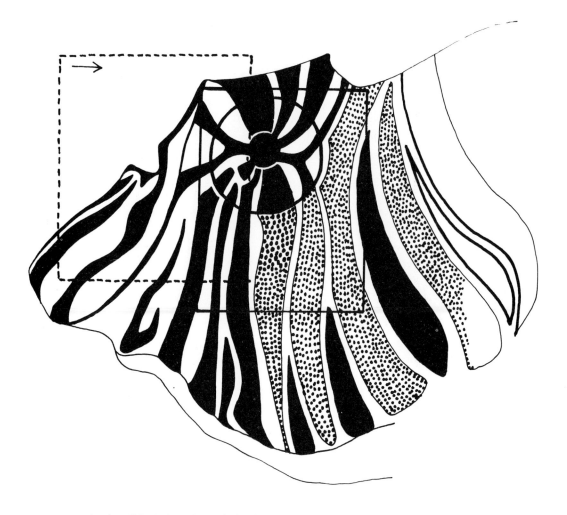

90a A simplified drawing of the head of a chameleon, showing the banded pattern radiating from the eye. As the eye swivels in all directions, so the bands move with it. Two rectangles have been placed over the design to capture interesting arrangements, which could be used in isolation as the basis for an abstract design

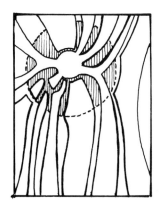

b In the most complex area of the design, the tones have been removed to show the quality of the lines rather than to emphasize the shapes. The design would be ideal for quilting, shadow quilting or goldwork

c Another area of the design needs more lines and deeper tones to achieve a better balance

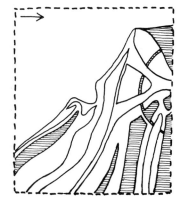

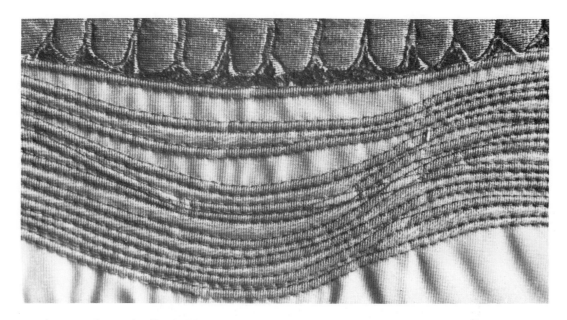

91 An experiment by Paula Templeman, inspired by skin patterns. English quilting and machined Italian quilting

92 Machine-embroidered textures by Maria Wetherall, inspired by the skin of a gecko. Beads have been used to create a denser area of colour across the centre

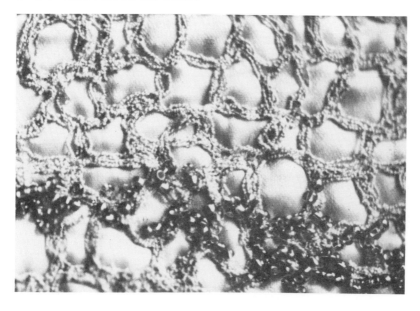

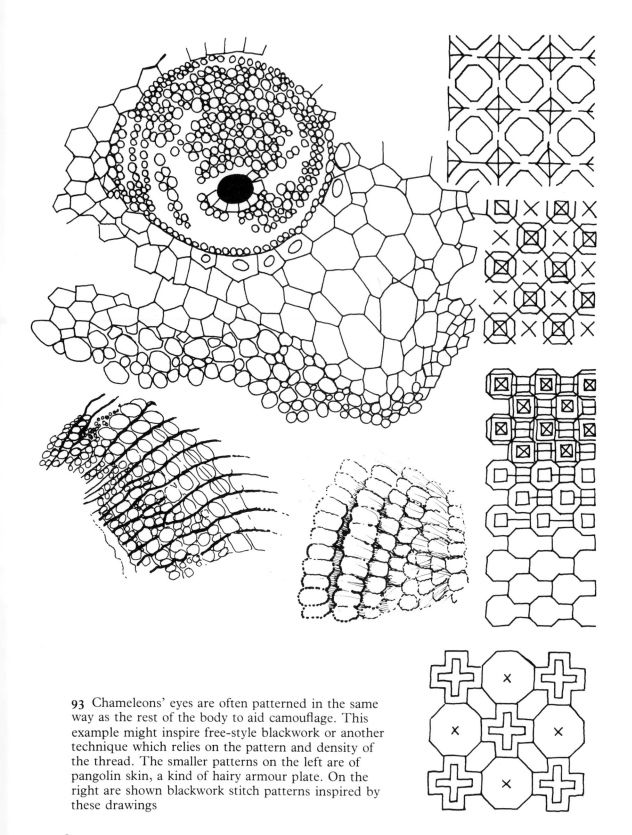

93 Chameleons' eyes are often patterned in the same way as the rest of the body to aid camouflage. This example might inspire free-style blackwork or another technique which relies on the pattern and density of the thread. The smaller patterns on the left are of pangolin skin, a kind of hairy armour plate. On the right are shown blackwork stitch patterns inspired by these drawings

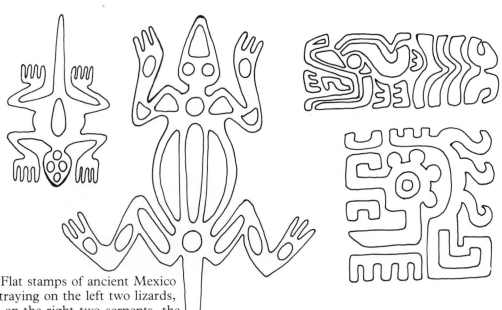

94 Flat stamps of ancient Mexico
portraying on the left two lizards,
and on the right two serpents, the
lower one plumed. These highly
stylized designs have been slightly
adapted during the re-drawing to
make them even more decorative.
They will translate perfectly into
many techniques, particularly
appliqué, quilting and shadow
work

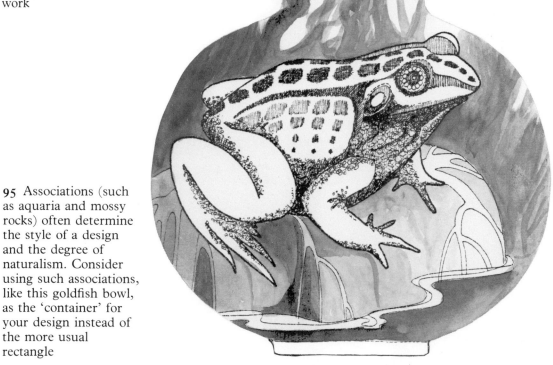

95 Associations (such
as aquaria and mossy
rocks) often determine
the style of a design
and the degree of
naturalism. Consider
using such associations,
like this goldfish bowl,
as the 'container' for
your design instead of
the more usual
rectangle

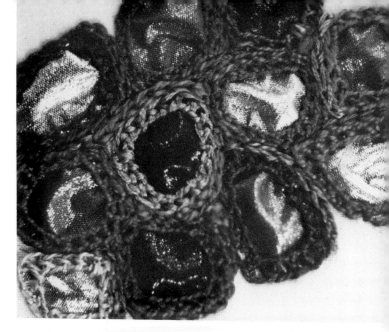

96 This small experiment by Mary Shea reproduces the texture and pattern of a crocodile skin, though it applies equally well to a frog or a toad. She uses padded lamé fabrics secured by buttonhole stitch in the manner of shisha glass, with chain stitch between

97 The compact shape of a tortoise makes an ideal, though unconventional box. Felt and leather, metallized cords and beads are some of the materials one could use on such a project

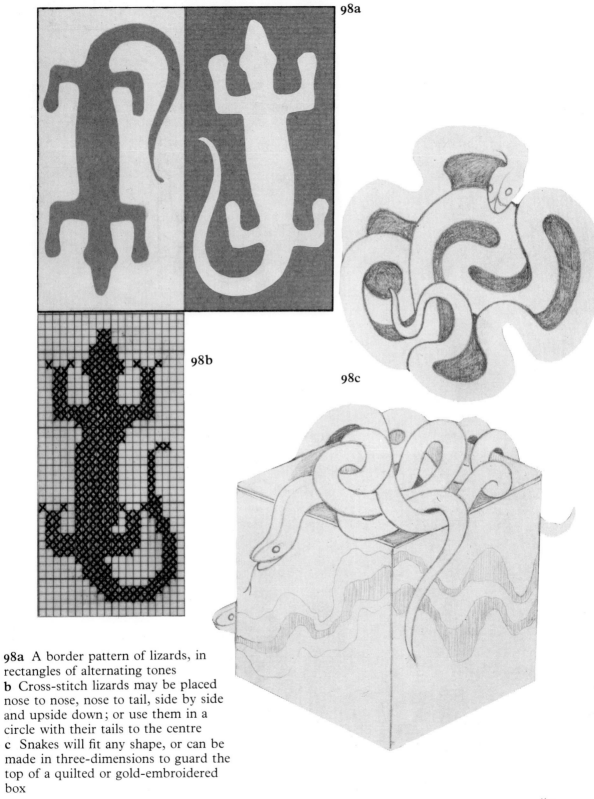

98a A border pattern of lizards, in
rectangles of alternating tones
b Cross-stitch lizards may be placed
nose to nose, nose to tail, side by side
and upside down; or use them in a
circle with their tails to the centre
c Snakes will fit any shape, or can be
made in three-dimensions to guard the
top of a quilted or gold-embroidered
box

99 Lizard, by Jane Wood. A large three-dimensional calico monster, highly textured with free smocking, beads and leather

100a 'Head of Medusa' by Heather Dorrough

b The 'hair' of snakes is removeable and becomes a collar. (*Photos: Heather Dorrough*)

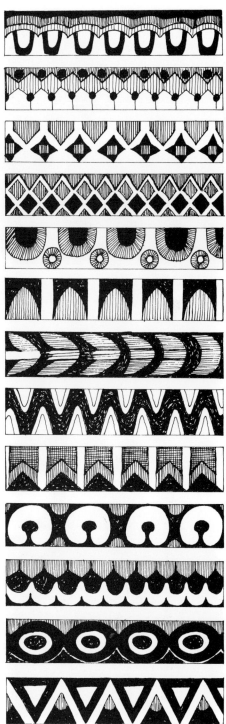

101 One of the best aspects of using snakes in design, apart from the adaptable shape, is the rich variety of patterns. Those seen here are all from snake skins, many of them in brilliant colours. They may be used in one large wall-hanging as they appear here, on a quilted bed cover or a felt-appliqué garment.

89

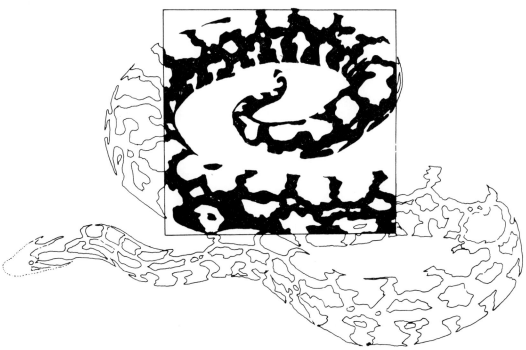

102 A snake pattern seen as both positive and negative.

Birds

Birds will adapt easily to both the simplest and the most complicated shapes. The easiest way to design with bird forms and one which a comparative beginner may find most useful, is to simplify the shape of a standing, sitting or swimming bird where the wings are laid against the body at rest. This will retain the decorative profile with wing and tail patterns included, without the added complexities of flight attitudes.

Designs based on birds in flight need careful study, as different species have entirely different outlines when their wings and bodies are in motion. In flight, wings and tail feathers extend to cover a much greater area, and the feather formation should bear some relationship to reality, taking full advantage of the beautiful patterns they create. Look at the birds in flight in figure 112 and note the various wing and tail positions, and the resulting variation in feather patterns.

In your observations on bird shapes and positions, make a careful note of such details as the way in which wings join onto the body, the shape of the tail, how the head comes from the neck, the legs and feet, and which way the leg joints bend. Beaks and eyes are also important details which help to give birds character and expression. Indeed, in the cases of the toucan, pelican, hornbill and flamingo the beak is all-important to the credibility of the design.

It is not essential to the design to place your bird in its natural environment, but the following list of associations may help to build a mental image before pencil reaches paper.

ASSOCIATIONS

Water birds: lakes, ponds, streams, the sea and shoreline, waves, rocks, reeds, grasses, fish.

Tall birds (e.g. heron, ostrich, flamingo): water (as above), roof tops, foliage, desert and scrubland, zoos and aviaries.

Domestic birds: cage, dovecote, nesting box, hen-house and broody box, pigeon loft, travel-basket, human hands, bird table, milk bottle, perch.

General: eggs, feathers, nest, tree branch or post, telegraph wires, roof tops and chimneys, clouds, sunset, moonscapes, baked in a pie, thieving magpie, pear-tree (partridge), bird in the hand.

103 Standing and sitting birds are easy to embroider when their wings are safely tucked away. A dovecote or similar construction instantly suggests doves and pigeons. This may be made as decorative as you wish or may quietly blend into the background while the more richly decorative treatment is used on the birds

OPPOSITE

104 A 'bird in the hand'—a racing pigeon sits calmly with its feet held gently behind it. Pigeons vary in colour-pattern and markings, making individuals easy to recognize. (*Photo: Vincent Morris*)

105 Rhea. Compare this head, neck and body with that of the pigeon. The feathers are also of an entirely different texture. (*Photo: Vincent Morris*)

106 Make a study of birds' heads to note the characteristic details of beaks, eyes, tufts of feathers and neck shapes. It is also important to study the claws

107 Mandarin Duck

108 'Bird on Nest' by Beryl Court. A richly decorated bird sits snugly on its nest of needleweaving. This is a perfect technique for suggesting twigs and foliage

109 On its wooden perch, this splendid macaw surveys visitors with interest as they pass. The massive beak on the large and powerful head is perfectly balanced by the very long tail and large claws

110 'Wol' by Anne Dyer. A 30 cm (12 in.) high, three-dimensional owl in canvaswork, using knitting wools and carpet thrums. (*Photo: A. Dyer*)

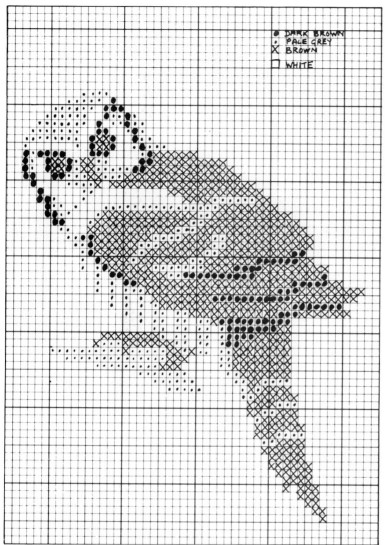

Key:
- ● DARK BROWN
- • PALE GREY
- X BROWN
- □ WHITE

III TOP: a similar design of an owl on its perch is here translated into a chart suitable for cross stitch. The colours may be of the embroiderer's own choice, or as indicated in the key BELOW: a swan and duck are charted for Assisi work, which leaves the design void, placing the stitches in the negative shapes

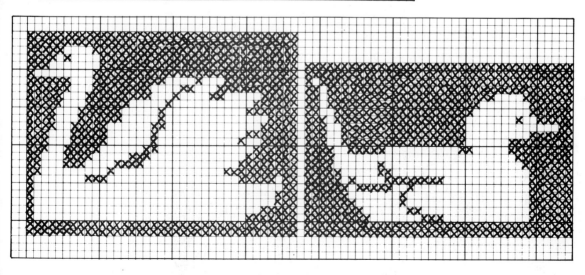

112 Birds in flight. Their shapes and attitudes vary greatly, so make careful observations before you begin your design

113
115

114

113 'The Galah' by Heather Dorrough. A bird in flight translated into machine quilting, showing the formation of the wing feathers from below. (*Photo: Heather Dorrough*)

114 'Golden Eagle' by Heather Dorrough. (*Photo: Heather Dorrough*)

115 Beautiful patterns seen on the back of a pheasant, each feather accentuated by black and white tips. The shadow of a wire fence may also be seen on its back, lending another pattern to the one already there

116 Turkeys showing off their magnificent wattles, textured hoods and rich brown feather patterns. Each feather is squared instead of rounded, creating an unusual effect on the backs

116

117 The hen is basically a very simple shape made of felt and canvaswork, with glittering pom-poms on the wings. The mouse is made in four sections with applied squares of felt and beads. (*Photo: Gail Bathgate*)

118 A design adapted from a photograph of a Bean Goose. The feather-patterns, especially those on the breast and neck, have been simplified to make them more suitable for those techniques demanding flowing lines such as goldwork, quilting or couching

119 Puffins

120 Penguins

121 Flocks of birds in silhouette

122 Tile designs by William de Morgan showing extravagant images of exotic birds, beasts and fish, suggest experiments to fit a design into a specific shape

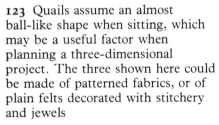

123 Quails assume an almost ball-like shape when sitting, which may be a useful factor when planning a three-dimensional project. The three shown here could be made of patterned fabrics, or of plain felts decorated with stitchery and jewels

124 BOTTOM RIGHT: a flat stamp from ancient Mexico
shows a highly stylized condor. Used in a bold manner as
befits the design, it could decorate a waistcoat, box or
wall-hanging. Motifs can be isolated from the original
design for use on different parts of the objects

125a This ceramic turkey soup tureen is the basis of a series of designs showing how one may simplify to achieve a number of different results

b The wing feathers are simplified but left intact. Everything else is smoothed out and left undetailed

c The straight lines still follow the original ones made by the edges of the feathers

d Four of the birds arranged in a square
e They may also be used as a border pattern

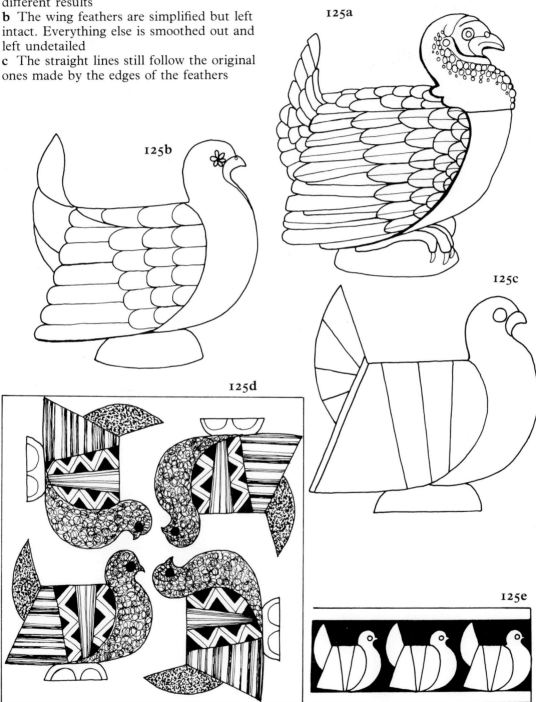

125a

125b

125c

125d

125e

126 Designs taken from ceramics, bronzes and museum sources are very useful to embroiderers as they are often already simplified. However, beware of using them exactly as they are; they will almost always need adapting in some way. The lower drawing is of an Indian Jungle Fowl

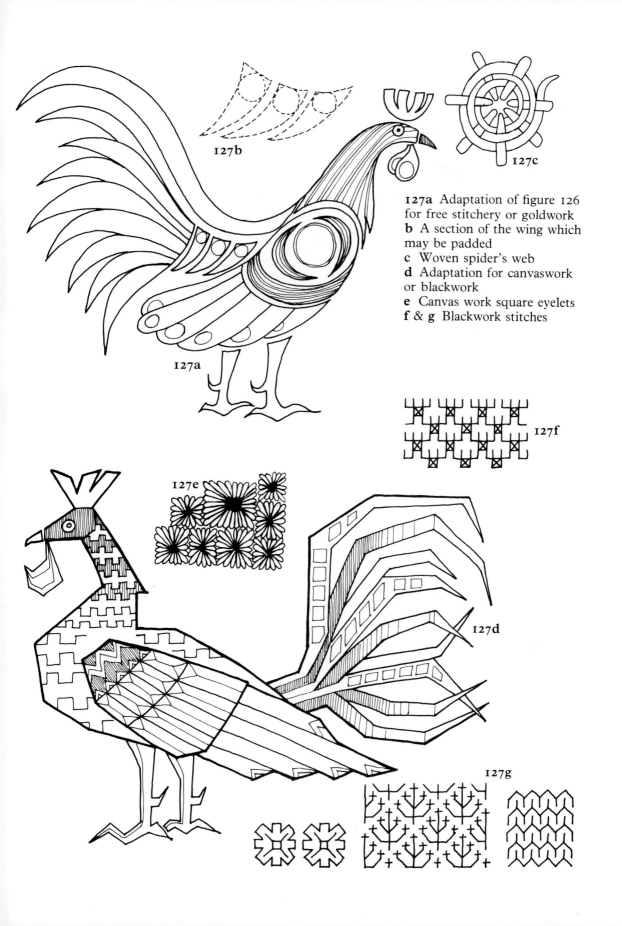

127a Adaptation of figure 126
for free stitchery or goldwork
b A section of the wing which
may be padded
c Woven spider's web
d Adaptation for canvaswork
or blackwork
e Canvas work square eyelets
f & **g** Blackwork stitches

127b

127c

127a

127f

127e

127d

127g

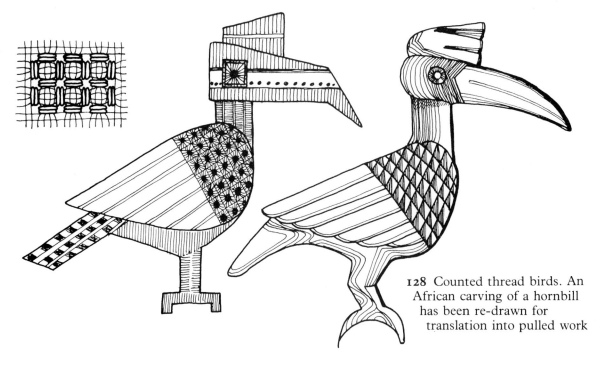

128 Counted thread birds. An African carving of a hornbill has been re-drawn for translation into pulled work

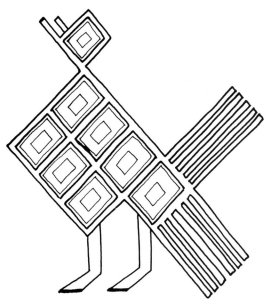

129 This little angular bird is a brocade-weave turkey from Guatemala, ideally adapted to the technique. It would adapt equally well to pulled work or canvaswork

130 Small, simple motifs charted for cross stitch. Two colours are used in the top one, but only one colour for the duck (except for the eye and beak)

Mammals

One may design a bird, a butterfly or a fish without a precise identification being necessary; any bird, butterfly or fish is quite acceptable, either in fact or in fancy. However, this does not seem to be the case with mammals; here it is important to most people that the animal portrayed is a specific one, even when rendered in its most symbolic form. Of course, instances occur of fantastic animals in myth, legend and heraldry, but even these have their own particular descriptions, names and idiosyncrasies. Perhaps the reason is that to invent a creature so far up in the hierarchy of the animal kingdom would be trying to out-do nature, or perhaps an invented animal makes us feel somewhat uncomfortable.

This being so, for whatever reason, most designers of embroidery (i.e. all of us who embroider) tend to prefer a certain type of creature, perhaps because their own favourite techniques adapt well in this way; delicate stitchery for small field-mice on ears of corn, heavily padded leather shapes for a muscular bull, or shimmering goldwork on a ceremonial elephant. It is inevitable that, sometimes unconsciously, we look for design material which suits our favourite technique as well as the type of project we have in mind. Bearing in mind the design section at the beginning of the book and the importance of capturing the essential ingredients of the animal, its spirit and character, consider the ideas below, which may remind you of some of the characteristic shapes.

Compact: pangolin, armadillo, porcupine, hedgehog, squirrel, rabbit, mouse, koala, panda, sitting and lying animals.
Solid: kangaroo, elephant, sheep, mountain goat, bull, bison, buffalo, rhinocerous, hippopotamus, seal, sea-lion.
Tall and leggy: horse, camel, monkey, antelope, giraffe, some dogs and cats.
Stripes and spots: zebra, tapir, deer, large and small cats, okapi, some horses.

The solid and compact shapes are particularly useful when creating three-dimensional embroideries as the amount of visible leg and neck is usually small, making basic construction easier.

ASSOCIATIONS
1 Wild animals: the natural environment, hippos wallowing, snow,

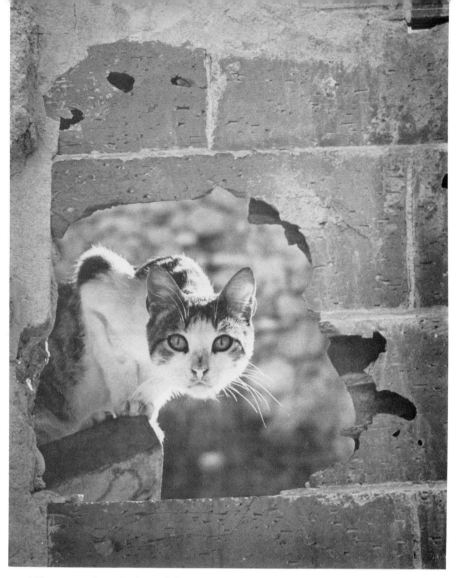

131 The natural curiosity of the cat was caught here in an instant as it took one quick look and bounded off. The roughened wall frames the cat's head and adds to the complete design. (*Photo: Vincent Morris*)

mountains, desert, cacti, zoos, bars of cage, Noah's Ark.

2 Domestic animals: dog and cat baskets, cat and mouse, cushions, chairs, fireside, picture frames, 'the cat who walked by himself', dogs on lead, pigs in sty, sheared sheep, horse in harness.

3 General: ceremonial animals, horse and elephant, circus, beasts of burden and draught animals.

Some mammals are rarely seen away from the rest of the herd, and indeed make more of an impression this way than when alone. Look for patterns made by herds, either against each other, as with zebras, or against their backgrounds, as with a circle of bison.

132 Domestic cats are relatively easy to study, being close at hand and willing centres of attention. Note the shape of the face particularly, as this is important in establishing the character. Seen from the back, the pattern on the fur creates an exciting design. Make a log-cabin frame for a small embroidered pet cat like the one shown here

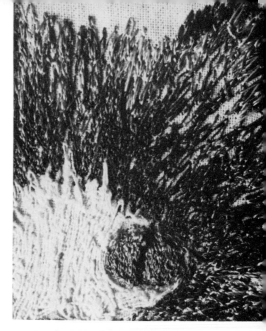

133 Knitted and crocheted cats by Jan Messent. Random-dyed and textured yarns create the patterns of cats' fur. Only the basic knit and crochet stitches have been used. (*By courtesy of the Knitting Craft Group*)

134 'Cat's Eye', by Sheila Read. Machine stitchery

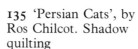

135 'Persian Cats', by Ros Chilcot. Shadow quilting

136 'Cat on Cushion', by Rosemary Jarvis. A more realistic type of cat with a patterned background'; the embroiderer has used straight stitches to suggest the smooth sheen of fur

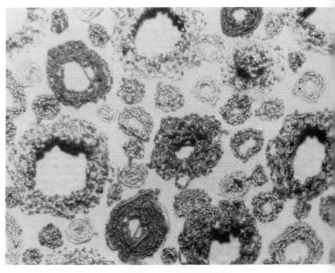

137 Wild cat's fur texture, by Maria Wetherall. Machine stitching on dyed fabric

138 Fur patterns and textures, by Mary Shea. Cutwork and machine embroidery

139 Wild cat. A very stylized drawing to emphasize the exciting pattern on the fur rather than its texture

140

141

140 & 141 Animal associations
140 A caged hare thinks of its freedom and its ghostly cousins
141 'Jugged Hare'. A whimsical interpretation in which the jug becomes part of the hare's natural surroundings

142a The ermine is a stoat in winter
clothing. Treat the background in a
decorative way, creating more texture
here than on the animal, to provide more
contrast with the smooth, white body
b Straight stitches used in blocks and at
random may be used for the background,
while ermine stitch also seems an
appropriate one to use

143 'Romney Marsh', by Barbara Hirst.
A three-dimensional sheep made of dyed
fabric strips and textured yarns, with the
head and limbs of felt

144

145

146

144 'Swaledale' by Valerie Hanson. Dyed fabric provides exactly the right misty background to this embroidery, which consists of loosely applied buttonhole stitch and couching. (*Photo: V. Hanson*)

145 Another sheep by Valerie Hanson has a closely-textured curly coat worked entirely in bullion knots. (*Photo: V. Hanson*)

146 Quilted calico sheep, by Clare Emery. The simplified padded shapes of the sheep catch the light exactly as sheep do when seen from a distance.

OPPOSITE
147 Sheep in folds during winter are seen from a distance as no more than bundles of wool, the light catching their backs. The rows of kale and the lines of hurdles provide a contrasting texture. (*By courtesy of the Institute of Agricultural History and Museum of English Rural Life, University of Reading*)

148 Cross stitch chart for a cow, pig, sheep and collie

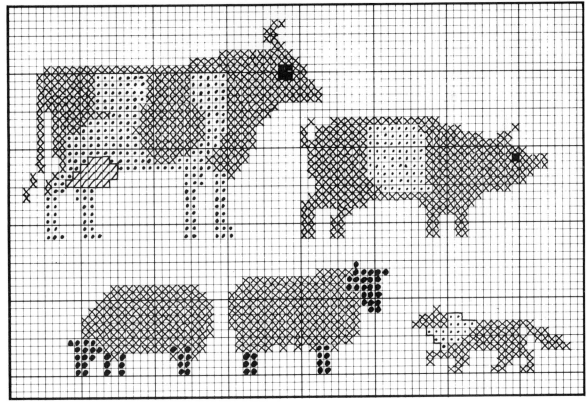

149 An eighteenth-century painting of a
heifer known as the Yorkshire Rose. The
exaggerated folds of skin make it an
interesting study for quilting. (*By courtesy
of the Institute of Agricultural History and
Museum of English Rural Life, University
of Reading*)

150 Note the different textures on the head of this heifer: damp leather, very hairy poll, heavy folds and smooth hair, also the swirl in the centre of the face. (*Photo: V. Morris*)

151 'Bull's Head', by Valerie Hanson. This embroidery captures perfectly the surly stare of the young bull as it peers around the tree. The whirlpool of hair on the face is achieved by straight stitches, as are the textures of the head and neck. (*Photo: V. Hanson*)

152 'Taurus', by Jane Lemon. Padded leather, gold kid and mottled fabric have been shaped and padded to follow the natural curves and contours of the body. The correct position of the lines accentuates the massive shoulders and buttocks. (*Photo: V. A. Campbell-Harding*)

153 'Bison', by Dorothy Stone. The heavy head and shoulders are covered with textured yarns and closely packed bullion knots to recreate the dense texture of the shaggy coat

154 A Brahma bull has long, loose folds of skin, huge floppy ears and large, sad eyes

155 'Bison', by Christine Andrews. A sturdy, three-dimensional animal made of suede, sheep's fleece and free stitchery

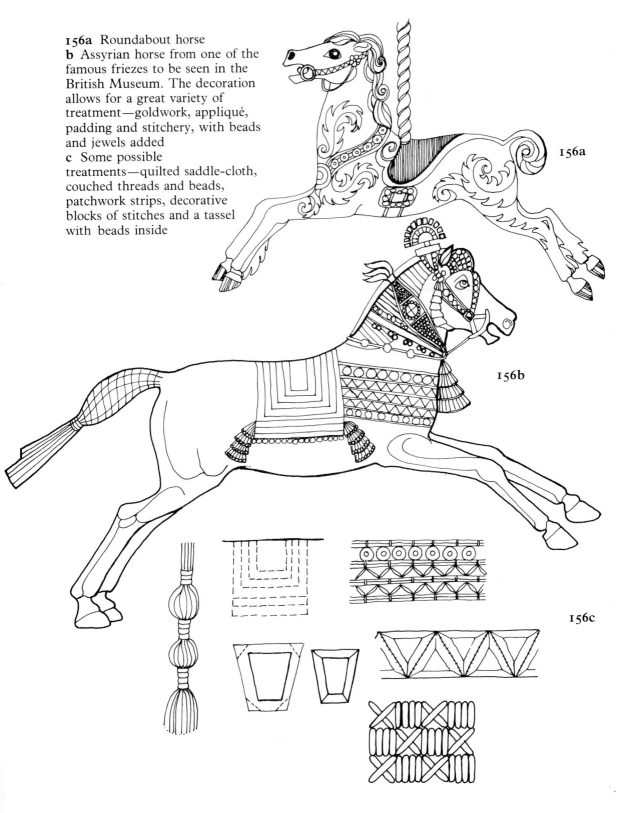

156a Roundabout horse
b Assyrian horse from one of the famous friezes to be seen in the British Museum. The decoration allows for a great variety of treatment—goldwork, appliqué, padding and stitchery, with beads and jewels added
c Some possible treatments—quilted saddle-cloth, couched threads and beads, patchwork strips, decorative blocks of stitches and a tassel with beads inside

156a

156b

156c

157a Chinese pottery horse, Tang Dynasty, *c.* seventh century, in the Victoria and Albert Museum, London. A stylized horse with massive body and neck, small head and an upright mane

b A figure from an Etruscan bronze bowl of *c.* 1000–500 BC. This angular design would adapt well to canvaswork or appliqué and padding
c Circus horse

158a Zebra's stripes vary not only from one breed to another, but also within the same breed. Points to note about zebras generally are that the head is quite large, the back flatter, the tail more like a cow's than a horse's and the ears large; the stripes extend into the erect mane. (*Photo: V. Morris*)
b The same photograph, reduced to lines, placed upside down and middle to middle, making an unusual line pattern parts of which may be suitable for quilting, couching and goldwork

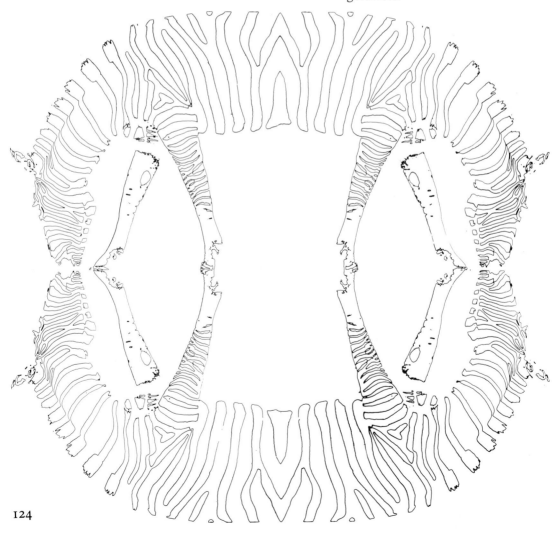

159 Pattern of stripes made by zebras' backs. Note how the stripe pattern continues down the tail on the right, and a 'Y' in the middle of the back. (*Photo: V. A. Campbell-Harding*)

160 BELOW Canvas embroidery zebra stripes, by Cherry Crawford

161 Zebra stripes undulate on the bodies according to the twist of the limbs. In these three examples, only the black parts of the animals have been drawn in, accentuating the pattern and showing how sometimes only parts of animals may be used to form a design

162 'Pirate', a beautifully marked horse painted in a very decorative manner to accentuate its worthiest features. (*By courtesy of the Institute of Agricultural History and Museum of English Rural Life, University of Reading*)

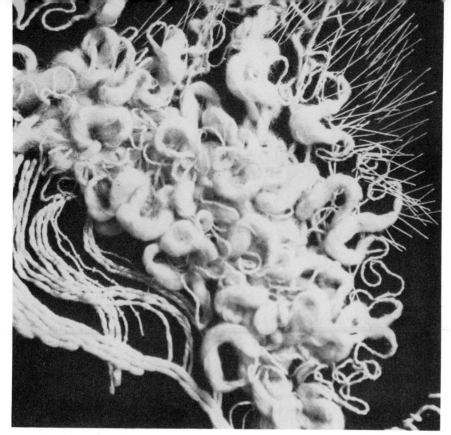

163a An experiment by Clare Emery to reproduce the texture of fur, using assorted threads in couching and straight stitches

b Paula Templeman's experiment also reproduces the tangle of a thick, furry coat like the camel's. She uses wrapped wire, couched onto a machine embroidered surface

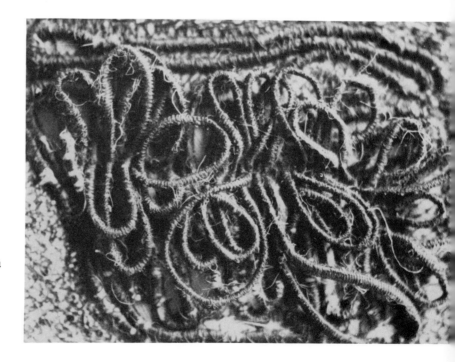

164 Bactrian camel. Note the furry top-knot on the head, the shaggy neck fur, the front 'leggings', the remarkably straight hind legs, the very long body and the small horizontal head carriage. (*Photo: V. A. Campbell-Harding*)

165 A little boar from ancient Greece shows the decorative lines accentuating the rippling muscles and the hairy mane which continues almost to the tail. In ancient times the boar was revered as a symbol of strength, courage and virility in many parts of the world and was adopted by men as a personal insignia

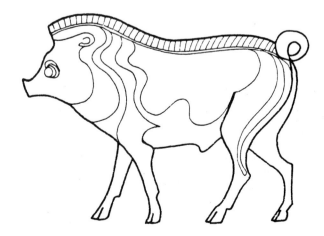

166

167

130

168a A beautiful giraffe, showing clearly the haughty expression and markings on the body and neck which become smaller and fainter at the extremities. (*Photo: V. A. Campbell-Harding*)

OPPOSITE
166 A semi-realistic Siamese cat on which much of the texture is decorative rather than realistic

167 All patterned animals have differently organized sets of markings. Some have solid spots, some hollow, some horse-shoe shaped and others more complex still. Study these carefully before you add 'spots' to your animal. Even giraffes have two distinct types of marks

b Sheila Read's experiment reproduces spots of the giraffe in machine embroidery surrounded by hand stitching

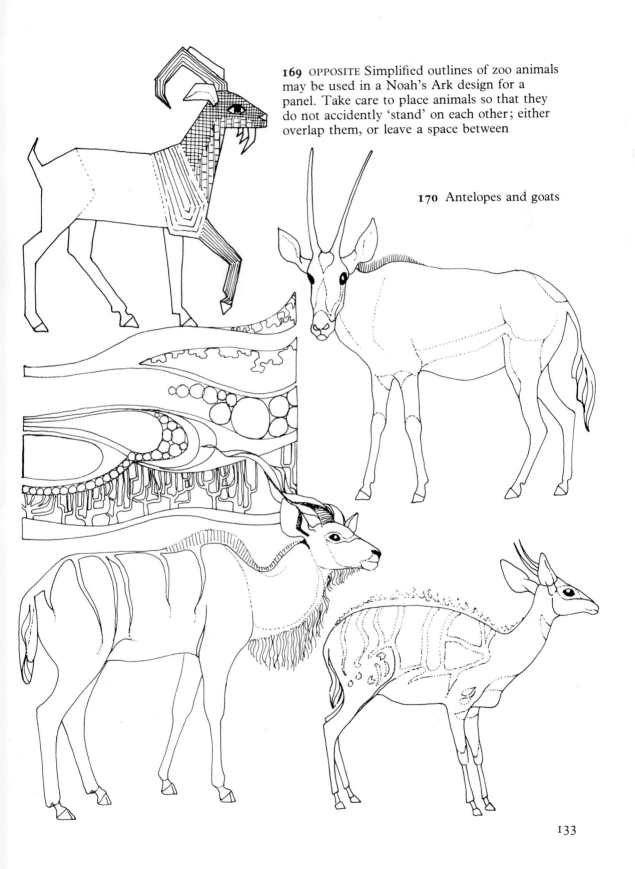

169 OPPOSITE Simplified outlines of zoo animals may be used in a Noah's Ark design for a panel. Take care to place animals so that they do not accidently 'stand' on each other; either overlap them, or leave a space between

170 Antelopes and goats

133

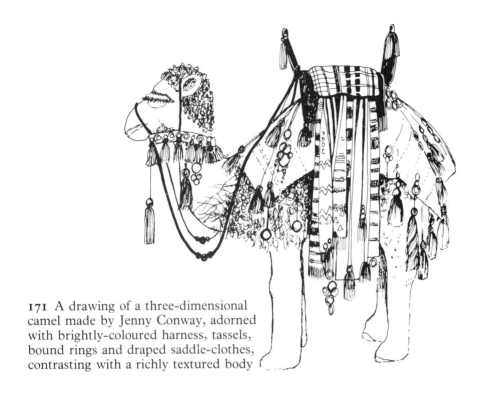

171 A drawing of a three-dimensional camel made by Jenny Conway, adorned with brightly-coloured harness, tassels, bound rings and draped saddle-clothes, contrasting with a richly textured body

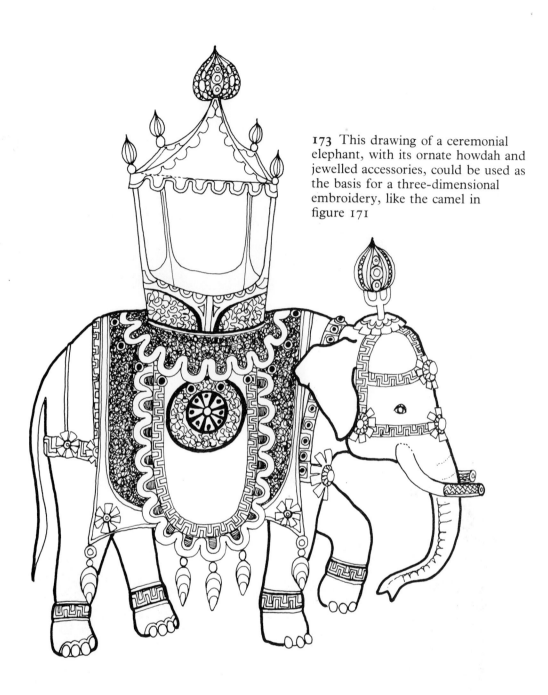

173 This drawing of a ceremonial elephant, with its ornate howdah and jewelled accessories, could be used as the basis for a three-dimensional embroidery, like the camel in figure 171

172 OPPOSITE: A three-dimensional elephant, by Mary Shea, completely covered in richly textured machine embroidery. The body is solid and stands firmly, and the skin glistens with lamé fabric underneath the stitching

174 'Three Elephants' Heads', by Clare Emery. Pattern darning on evenweave linen

175 Three samples of textures derived from parts of an elephant
a Heavy stitching over folds of fabric, with velvet ribbon, by Paula Templeman
b Bound rolls of fabric to suggest the trunk texture, by Mary Shea
c Pleating and padding to suggest an elephant's eye, by Jane Wood

175a

175b

175c

176 'Hippo's Head', by Sheila Read. The quilted mask of a hippo shows a variety of textures from the lined and padded eyes and cheeks to smocked forehead and whiskered nose

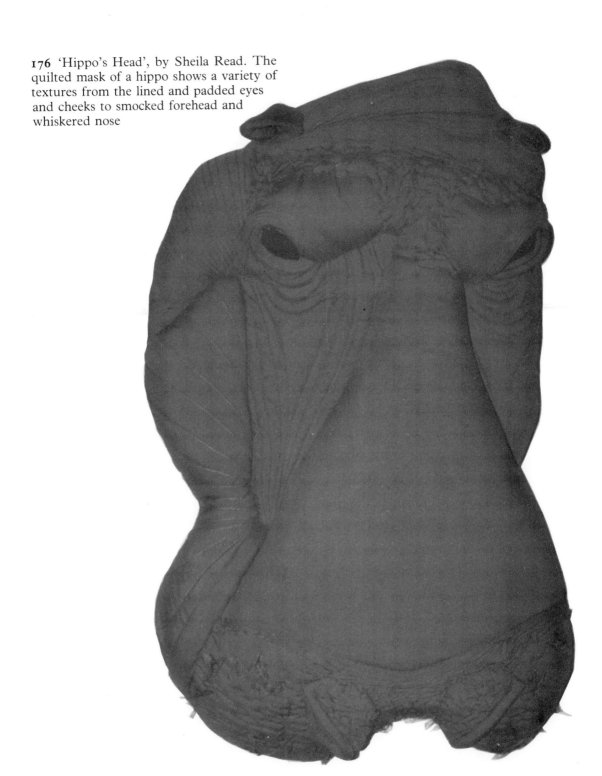

177a Albrecht Dürer's well-known drawing of a rhino is perhaps another case of an animal being described to the artist rather than one drawn directly from life. However, it does provide an excellent basis for design, as the lower drawing shows.

b This design is a drawing of a three-dimensional rhino (called Rumbold) made by Joan Hake, and based on Dürer's drawing. It shows how easily the patterns may be translated with a little adaptation

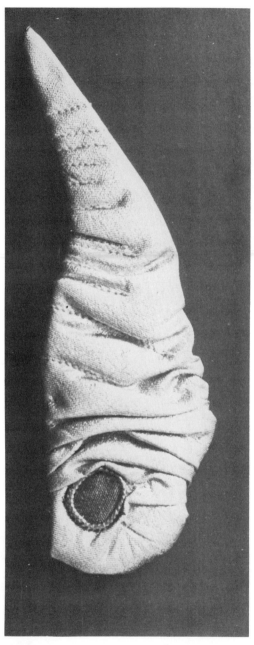

178 Rhino horn, by Sheila Read. An experiment to reproduce the folds and ridges using a gold-thread fabric and stitchery

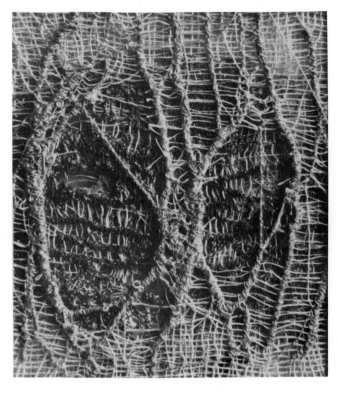

179 Two experiments based on
animal skins which may be used
on an embroidered rhino, taking
Dürer's drawing as a model
a Pulled-work on loose scrim, by
Maria Wetherall
b Pulled-work on hessian, by
Sheila Read

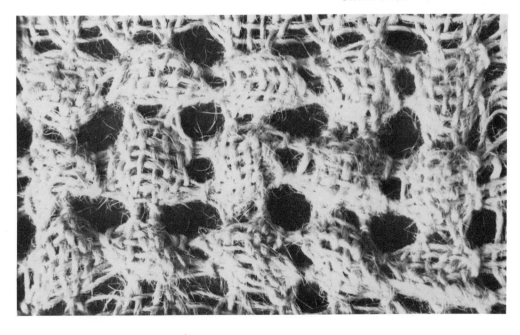

Bibliography

GENERAL EMBROIDERY

Jones, Nora, *Embroidery* (Guidelines series), Macdonald Educational 1978
Phillpott, Pat, *The Craft of Embroidery*, Stanley Paul 1976
Whyte, Kathleen, *Design in Embroidery*, Batsford 1983

HERALDRY

Child, Heather, *Heraldic Design*, G. Bell & Sons 1965
Mackinnon, Charles, *The Observer's Book of Heraldry*, Warne 1966
Miller, Carey, *Monsters and Mysterious Beasts*, Pan Books 1974

INSECTS

Seguy, E. A., *Decorative Butterflies and Insects*, Dover, New York 1977

BIRDS

Jonsson, Lars, *Birds of Lake, River, Marsh and Field*, Penguin 1979
Jonsson, Lars, *Birds of Mountain Regions*, Penguin 1979
The World Atlas of Birds, Mitchell Beazley 1974

FISH

Abbott, R. Tucker, *Seashells*, Bantam Books 1976
Cooper, Allan, *Fishes of the World*, Hamlyn 1969

REPTILES

Stidworthy, John, *Snakes of the World*, Hamlyn 1969

MAMMALS

Alderson, Lawrence, *The Observer's Book of Farm Animals*, Warne 1976
Classification of the Animal Kingdom, English Universities Press 1973
Metcalf, Christine, *Cats*, Hamlyn 1969
Osmond, Edward, *Wild Cats*, World Distributors Ltd

Suppliers

UK

The Campden Needlecraft Centre, High Street, Chipping Campden, Gloucestershire

S. N. Cooke Ltd., 18 Wood Street, Stratford-on-Avon, Warwickshire

The Handicraft Shop, 5 Oxford Road, Altrincham, Cheshire

The Handworker's Market, 6 Bull Street, Holt, Norfolk NR25 6HP

Mace and Nairn, 89 Crane Street, Salisbury, Wiltshire SP1 2PY

Needle and Thread, 80 High Street, Horsell, Woking, Surrey

The Nimble Thimble, 26 The Green, Bilton, Rugby CV22 7LY

Richmond Art and Craft, Dept. E1, 181 City Road, Cardiff CF2 3JB

Christine Riley, 53 Barclay Street, Stonehaven, Kincardineshire AB3 2AR

Royal School of Needlework, 25 Princes Gate, London SW7 1QE

Spinning Jenny, Bradley, Keighley, West Yorkshire BD20 9DD

Teazle Embroideries, 35 Boothferry Road, Hull HU3 6UA

USA

Appleton Brothers of London, West Main Road, Little Compton, Rhode Island 02837

American Crewel Studio, Box 298, Boonton, New Jersey 07005

American Thread Corporation, 90 Park Avenue, New York

Bucky King Embroideries, Box 371, King Bros, 3 Ranch Buffalo Star Rte, Sheridan, Wyoming 82801

Craft Kaleidoscope, 6412 Ferguson Street, Indianapolis 46220

Dharma Trading Company, 1952 University Avenue, Berkeley, California 94704

The Golden Eye, Box 205, Chestnut Hill, Massachusetts 02167

Heads and Tails, River Forest, Illinois 60305

Lily Mills, Shelby, North Carolina 28150

Threadbenders, 2260 Como Avenue, St Paul, Minnesota 55108

The Thread Shed, 307 Freeport Road, Pittsburgh, Pennsylvania 15215

CANADA

Sutton Yarns, 2054 Yonge Street, Toronto, Ontario

Leonida Leatherdale Embroidery Studio, 90 East Gate, Winnipeg, Manitoba R3C2C3

Index